GRADUALLY TO GOD

Gradually To God

Published by One Drop Media
Wilmington, North Carolina USA

Printed in the United States

ISBN 978-0-615 4450-3-8

First Edition
April, 2011

Praise for Gradually to God

"As the son of a pastor I know all about 'conversion' experiences that give us bragging rights—when we can name the time and place when our lives were dramatically transformed. In Gradually to God Doug presents an equally authentic approach to knowing God—that of gaining insights, confidence and faith that come over time. It gave me a renewed peace about my own history and growth as a believer. "

—Dan Miller, Author of
48 Days to the Work You Love

"Doug Wahl is passionate. He's passionate about life, about relationships and most importantly he is passionate about God. In this book you will enjoy hearing his story of faith and doubt, joy and misery, and how these emotions affected his journey toward God. It wasn't easy—it never is. And it didn't happen overnight—it rarely does. But in this raw and real memoir, you get a front row seat viewing of Doug's gradual steps of faith."

—Jason Malec
New Denver Church

"Gradually to God is a book with great insight into a REAL journey with God. It is a thought provoking and honest book that shows believers and nonbelievers alike that God is listening and desires to have an ongoing relationship with us."

—Wade Morris
Wade Morris Ministries

"Doug's journey to God is very real, whether you are Christian, Buddhist, Muslim, Jew or practice Native American Spirituality. Wahl takes us on a bittersweet ride that shows the ups and down; ins and outs of finding spiritual confidence and peace."

—Deanna Sauceda
Anchor KRQE News 13 Albuquerque, New Mexico

"Gradually to God isn't just one man's story, it's a person's guide to a clearer understanding of God—a work book of faith. A no-nonsense account of real life, raw emotion and how hitting rock bottom can actually spring-load your life towards greatness. No matter where you are on the faith-scale, Gradually to God balances out a lot of unanswered questions."

—Adam Williams
Anchor personality Boston, Massachusetts

"Doug Wahl's ability to draw you into the situations in this book where you can actually feel in both your heart and mind what's happening is amazing. A truly gifted writer and a book you won't want to put down. A must read."

—Ashley Morrison
Business Anchor-CBS News

Gradually to God

By
Doug Wahl

One Drop Media
Wilmington, NC USA

For my son Brody: Without you,
this walk would have never gotten started.

For my friend Adrienne: Without you,
this book would have never been completed.

"Reaching people and helping them walk with God."

Mission Statement,
Port City Community Church
Wilmington, North Carolina

FOREWORD

YOU WILL LIKE THIS BOOK. It's not just Doug's story. It is your story. It's my story. In a way, it's everyone's story. It doesn't really matter at what age your faith was born because the process is always gradual.

You should have seen me at sixteen. I was a mess. I was not at all the person I wanted to be. Worse yet, there was nowhere for me to turn. If I confided in others, my parents or church friends, they'd just come to the conclusion that I wasn't a real believer.

And so I tried to deal with it on my own. Occasionally, I'd go to the woods surrounding our neighborhood and sit there until my eyes filled-up with tears. How did it come to this? I had been a Christian half of my life, but I felt like such a fraud and a fake.

Part of the problem was my thoughts. They weren't always pure. Few people knew about that little secret. But they were becoming more aware of the other issue—my mouth—which had developed a liking for swear words. Neither of these were concerns when I accepted Christ at the age of seven—so what went wrong? Is it possible that my conversion wasn't real? That it didn't take?

I knew Jesus had forgiven me and come inside my life to help me live more like Him. But I kept finding myself thinking the same thoughts, speaking the same words over and over again. What kind of follower was I?

Then I discovered that the apostle Paul struggled with the same thing—well, maybe not cussing or impure thoughts, but clearly something was bothering him. He writes in his letter to the Romans; “For I do not do what I want, but I do the very thing that I hate.” There was a verse I could really relate to. But what could I do? It all seemed so futile. Part of me simply wanted to give up.

But rather than give up, I simply paid attention. I begin to notice that amid my doubt there was faith. I begin to see that the questions that I had about myself, that made me ashamed, opened my eyes to seeing God in ways that I had never seen him before. I begin to sense that even with all the disappointment and self criticism that I was being changed—gradually.

I discovered that my faith was not a destination at which I arrived, but a process by which I was being formed to be more like Christ. Years later, when I started a church in Wilmington, North Carolina, I wanted to focus on helping people take steps in that direction by simply concentrating on doing the next right thing.

Doug Wahl found his way to the middle school where our church was meeting. It was right in the middle of a series I was teaching on the book of Job. It turned out to be the perfect time for him.

I remember our first encounter. He had a subtle swagger and a bit of cockiness. His words were few, and even though they revealed a methodical thinker, it was clear that he couldn’t really explain what he felt.

After the service, he approached me. "You are very good at what you do but I am not sure I learned anything today..." There was a slight pause, as though he were uncertain if he should amend his position, but then added, "I'll be back next week."

I had no idea of the process that Doug would step into and walk through over the next five years. But I know that Doug's story confirms what the Bible says and what I came to believe as a high school student struggling with my issues. Doug's journey confirms that God finishes what He starts. God uses every moment and every experience. Through joy and pain, fulfillment and disappointment, God wastes nothing as He draws us to Himself.

I have met few people who have embraced the process with as much tenacity and reflection as Doug. This book will make you laugh. It will make you think. It will make you wonder, but it ultimately gives you hope. Hope in the promise that God is faithful to complete every good work He begins. You will find in the pages to follow the way in which God draws those far from Him into His presence and how God deals with those who draw near. But most of all, you will find yourself. You will find that the starts and stops, the promises and broken promises are all part of the journey.

You will find that doubt and fear and faith are woven together in a process by which you are formed into the Image of the One of which you are made. You will find that with each step and each moment, you are being changed and renewed, restored and redeemed... that you are being forged, and finally, that you are ultimately being drawn... Gradually to God.

Mike Ashcraft
Senior Pastor
Port City Community Church

PREFACE

DOUBT

"I am still not all I should be,
but I am focusing all my energies on this one thing:
forgetting the past and looking forward
to what lies ahead."
(Philippians 3:13-14 NLT)

THE U-TURN

I know it doesn't make much sense to begin a book in this manner, especially not a Christian book. Most manuscripts written about faith are composed with the hope that the final product will help the reader grow spiritually. To those authors, a relationship with God is all about direction. It's about the fork in the road, choosing the right path, starting a journey and taking the next step in the walk.

They're right of course. In fact I share the same ambition; maybe something recorded here will help you along the way.

But I also have to tell you about the U-Turn.

There was a moment in time when all forward progress for me came to a sudden and screeching stop. I was literally required to change course and start heading back to where I had just escaped.

The redirection was a result of a cruel text message: "Don't bother coming," it told me. "We're in Louisiana."

I know that doesn't make sense to you. Hopefully it will by the end of the book, but for right now the message was confirmation that my biggest fear was coming true.

As my car got on the off ramp, exiting the interstate, and then on the overpass which lead me to the opposite side of the expressway, I had to wonder if the giant U-Turn was really symbolic of something more. After all this time, was it possible for me to change the larger course of my life and head back to the place where I came from?

For four years I had been calling myself a Christian, but this is not what I had signed up for. Far from it! In fact I had turned to God in the first place in the hopes that He would prevent this text message from ever being sent. And now, after all this time, of faithful church attendance, prayer, journaling, small group meetings and volunteering, it was delivered anyway. What was the point to it all?

Something inside me tried to answer that question with a passage from Philippians. The Bible tells us to focus all our energy on forgetting the past and looking forward to what's ahead.

Ahead?

That's impossible when you're in the process of turning around.

The change in direction forced me to think about the past—like it or not. It seemed like a memory from the last few years was coming to life with each back-tracked mile. They were playing out in reverse chronological order. If you read this book starting with the end and worked your way to the beginning, you'd get some sense of my thought process.

Some of the memories, the nicer ones, confirmed in my heart that there was a God who had everything under control. But other images only increased my fears and doubts. The text message started a major crisis of faith. It was becoming hard to believe that following Jesus was really getting me anywhere.

By the time the pointless round-trip was over, my mind had also completed its journey. Reaching for the car door handle, I flashed back to the final memory. It happened years earlier, but remained so vivid. I could clearly see the face of a broken man who sat in another car parked in another time and place. For him, the question that day was whether he'd finally have the courage to open the door and start walking.

I guess it probably makes a lot more sense to start the story there.

PART 1

THE RETURN

"Get to know the God of your ancestors.
Worship and serve him with your whole
heart and mind. For the Lord sees every heart
and knows every plan and thought. If you seek Him
you will find Him."
(1 Chronicles 28:9 NLT)

"If you return to me and obey my commands,
even if you are exiled to the ends of the earth,
I will bring you back to the place I have chosen
for my name to be honored."
(Nehemiah 1:9)

1

The Prodigal Son

Junior high sucked the first time around! At least it did for me. I am assuming it did for you. I don't know anyone who looks back at those three years as the best in their life. For most of us, that period was one big era of confusion. And now, for me, a man in his mid-thirties, somehow I was about to re-enter that world.

The feeling of awkwardness was all around me. It all came rushing back one Sunday morning while sitting in my car, parked outside of a middle school. Once again it felt like I didn't fit in, that I'd never be accepted by the clique or the cool kids, that I was destined to be an outsider. The only thing missing was the acne, but the receding hairline and expanding waistline provided the same kind of physical insecurity.

Every weekend in Wilmington, North Carolina, a conversion of sorts takes place. Actually, a similar routine plays out across America, in cities and towns where the school district wants to make a few extra bucks. On Friday afternoons, gangly pre-teenagers take their raging hormones and head home for the weekend…leaving their school to be rented out by evangelical Christians.

"So much for the separation of church and state," I sarcastically mumbled to myself. "You'd think these Bible-thumpers could spend some of the money they stashed away from not paying taxes and construct their own building. Put up a steeple! Make an altar out of gold, for all I care! Just stay out of our schools!"

Attending a religious service was not normally part of my weekend agenda. Church had been successfully avoided for the better part of two decades, except for the occasional funeral or wedding when social customs required an appearance.

Death was always the biggest test for this Atheist. How impossible it was not to roll my eyes when a preacher tried to console a grieving family: "He's in a better place now." Or "this was all part of God's plan." It all sounded so trite.

At weddings, the challenge came from trying to hold back my laughter. "Let no man put asunder what God has brought together." God? Really, God is responsible for this match? These two met at a bar! Jose Cuervo brought them together!

Those exceptions aside, God's place in my life was otherwise non-existent. And it would have stayed that way—should have stayed that way—if it weren't for a few unforeseen bumps in the road.

In large part, it was the unwanted influence of others that forced me to give church, religion and even God another try. Certainly I could blame the mother of my child. She recently dumped me, creating a broken heart, a search for answers and a desire to make sense of it all.

My Catholic parents were also at fault. Their concern was for their grandson's future and how he'd be raised in a broken home. "You should think about going back to church," they advised. "Brody needs some stability in his life right now."

The pure Machiavellian counsel of an attorney provided a different type of motivation: "Son, you live in the Bible Belt now," he told me during an initial meeting. "If you ever want to fight for custody, you need to get in good with God."

There was also an intrusive stranger, who for some unknown reason, chose to approach me while I was swimming at the neighborhood pool. "You're new to the area. Welcome! Looking for a church? You should try mine. It's just down the road at Roland Grise Middle School."

Perhaps more than anyone else, one person was responsible for getting me out of bed on a Sunday morning. A young co-worker spoke with wisdom far beyond his years. After hearing about the man at the pool, my friend followed up the stranger's advice with his own endorsement, "Hey, that's my church. You should go. Wait until you see all the good-looking women there!"

His words made sense—at least they did at first—but now sitting in my car, looking at the beautiful women as they walked into the school, only reminded me of how truly ugly my situation had become. I felt worse, not better. Where's the healing that everyone talks about? People recommend church as if it is some magic wand that can instantly correct your life. They never bother to talk about how much you'll feel isolated and out of touch.

This really was junior high all over again.

Every part of me wanted to put the keys back in the ignition and take off with gravel spitting out behind my tires. Somehow, against my better judgment, that didn't happen. I am not sure that I was fully conscious of it, but the car door was suddenly open and my feet were touching the pavement. It was a short distance between where I parked and the front door, but it took a lifetime to start the walk.

HURDLE: MY PARENTS' GOD

The phrase "freedom of religion" always bothered me. It certainly did not exist in my family's home. My parents never gave me list of options: "Son, would you like to be a Methodist? How about a Baptist? If you choose Judaism you'll get to wear one of those hats."

Religion isn't something you pick; it is something you inherit. Parents pass down their faith, or lack thereof, to their children who really can't do anything about it until they become adults. In short, I was Catholic because Mom and Dad were Catholic.

In fact it seemed like the entire world, or at least my childhood version of it, was Catholic. My neighborhood, my school, my Little League team were all dominated by Catholic children. We celebrated each other's first communions and confirmations. We were given medallions of saints to wear around our necks and instructed to give up something like ice cream for Lent. Our faith had less to do with going to church and more to do with being part of a community.

The Church still has a hold on me. It's been decades since I've attended a Mass, but if I went today it would all instantly come back. I'd know when to sit, when to stand, when to kneel, when to make the sign of the cross and when to shake hands with those sitting around me: "Peace be with you."

This was my parent's God. Yes, as an Atheist I broke free, but their way of worship remains my vision of what it looks like to have a relationship with a higher power. Anything outside of those rituals sounds like a like foreign language to me.

ON THE INSIDE, everything about Port City Community Church seemed so strange and even inappropriate. The congregation looked nothing like the typical gathering of churchgoers. They more resembled the middle school students who occupied the building during the week. Everyone was dressed in the most casual of clothes. The men were in shorts and T-shirts. The women were in sun dresses that showed off the type of tan you can only get in a town surrounded by beaches.

The customary wooden pews were replaced by individual theater seats. The walls were different too. Instead of gazing at the sun's rays as they peaked through the multi-colored stained glass, I'd be forced to stare at powder-blue cinder blocks.

All of these changes were reminders of how much I didn't belong, and I had no intentions of staying. In fact my feet were stepping back into the aisle, about to walk right out the door, when blaring music stopped them in their tracks.

Beginnings are important. Certain things in life really should have a formal opening. It's easy to tell when a wedding gets underway, when a sporting event kicks off, when a court proceeding starts: "All rise. The honorable Judge So-and-So is now presiding." Shouldn't a church service also have a beginning? There in the crowded auditorium, with people breaking out in song all around me, I discovered that at some point since my departure the church service had morphed into a music concert.

"Are you ready to rock, Wilmington!?"

Well, they didn't actually say that, but all of a sudden a grungy group of twenty-somethings took the stage. They made up a six-piece band, with two guitarists, a drummer, someone on the keyboard, a lead singer, with a back-up female vocalist.

"BLESSED BE THE NAME OF THE LORD. BLESSED BE HIS NAME, JEEEEEE-SUS!"

The lead singer was screaming into the microphone while the Jimmy Hendrix wannabe jammed alongside him. "Now the drum solo! Take it away, Ringo!"

I was forced from my seat the moment the woman in front of me stood up. Everyone was on their feet now. Some undoubtedly knew the words by heart, but if they didn't, all they had to do was follow the bouncing ball. The lyrics were plastered on two huge projection screens that flanked both sides of the stage.

"BLESSED BE THE NAME OF THE LORD, BLESSED BE YOUR GLORIOUS NAME."

A man in the front row raised one of his hands. His palm was flat and it faced directly forward. He looked as if he was trying to stop traffic. Within a split second another hand went up, and then another, and then another one after that. They were all from people sitting in the first half of the auditorium…. which gave their collective action the appearance that a mosh pit was forming. I started to wonder if the lead singer was going to dive into the outstretched arms. Meanwhile, my fingers were firmly stuck in the front pockets of my jeans only making me stick out like a sore thumb even more.

"Who's the new guy?" I could almost hear the inner thoughts of the flock, "Why isn't he singing along? Why aren't his hands lifted in praise? What does he have against Jesus?"

When the music finally stopped, we were encouraged to say "hello" to someone sitting around us.

"Hi. I'm Jim. This is my wife Susie," said the all-American couple behind me.

"I'm Doug," I responded with a flimsy and unconfident handshake. "Peace be with you?"

Jim and Susie were typical of the Port City crowd: young, white, on the preppy side. Many were college age. Several were in their late twenties or early thirties. There were only a handful of people in their forties, but virtually no one was older than that.

They were a handsome bunch. Even though none of them flaunted money, it was a gathering of people who seemed to have it all. Regardless of their casual dress, somehow they appeared to be in their Sunday best. As individuals, they were all probably nice—the type of people you'd want in the cubicle or the house next to yours. Still, as a group, I instantly hated every single one of them.

HURDLE: THE FUTURE IS NOW

The information page, on a popular social website, gives you a quick update on the life of any old acquaintance. It's all there in bullet points: hobbies, favorite music or television shows, relationship status, children, political views and so forth.

There's a woman I know who responded to those questions with a very sarcastic tone. My favorite of her answers came on the topic of religion: "With my party lifestyle??? Are you kidding me??? They won't let me anywhere near a church, LMAO!!"

I think a lot of people can relate to how she feels. It is not that my friend doesn't believe in God, it's just that she feels she's not good enough for Him. For whatever reason, she sees herself being unqualified, as someone who "need not apply." For so many people there is a great pressure to be godly before they have a relationship with God.

THE LEADER of the Port City cult is the church's senior pastor. If you called Central Casting and asked for someone to play a southern preacher, Mike Ashcraft would not be sent in your direction. He's more apt to get a few auditions for the romantic lead on a daytime soap opera.

He's got American Idol good looks, a full head of jet black hair, a slender build, and is always dressed casually right down to the flip-flops on his feet. He looks much younger than his age, which is thirty-six.

His sermon this morning is on the book of Job. Even though it's one of the most famous stories in the Bible, the details are unfamiliar to me.

It's basically about a bet made between God and Satan. The Devil argues that anyone can walk by faith when life is drama-free. If, on the other hand, bad things are allowed to happen, then believers will eventually lose their way.

Job, a very wealthy man, becomes the guinea pig for the wager. In a short period, he loses his money, his children, and is inflicted with a horrible and painful illness. His faith bends under the pressure, but he doesn't break. He remains a man of God. In the end, Satan loses the bet.

The story hit home. It was all so bizarre, so surreal. As much as I didn't belong, there was now this undeniable feeling that somehow I was supposed to be here—in this middle school auditorium—at this exact moment in time.

It seemed like the ancient story was being rewritten in my modern day life. Call it the Book of Doug. In fact, I wondered if any of the Bible thumpers sitting around me, or even the hip, young pastor on stage, could really relate to it as much as I did. What did they know about struggles? How could they really understand the pain and suffering that this man endured? Did they ever have a broken heart? Were their finances ever in ruin? Did they know what it was like to have all their dreams slip away? The smiling, worry-free, God-loving faces in the room told me the answer. Of course not!

As the service was coming to an end, part of me wanted to trade places with these believers. It wasn't that I had become one of them, not at all; it's just that I wanted the same smooth journey. These bumps in the road were getting kind of old.

And so, becoming a churchgoer got on my list of things to do. Oh, not right away of course. There was a lot of stuff to take care of first: the sinning, the beer, the language… I guess I should also be nicer to people. Maybe after all that was accomplished—just maybe—I could become a man of God. Heck, if I managed to do all that, maybe I would even start believing in Him, too.

Confession: The Real Reason I Went Looking for God

You want to know why I didn't believe in a higher power? It's simple, really. It just seemed like the concept of God was a little too convenient.

As humans, we need Him to ease the pain of death; either from losing a loved one or the fear of our own immortality.

Society needs Him to keep order. Without a divine providence to sit in judgment of our actions, we would have total anarchy.

Nations need Him to go to war. Young men and women do not risk their lives and futures unless they believe that by fighting, they are doing God's work.

Justice needs Him because too often bad things happen to good people. It only seems fair that someone is there to make sure it all equals out in the end.

The need for God is so great and so evident that throughout my adult life I argued that if a creation happened, it was us creating Him and not the other way around.

Then something eventually happened, something that would make me the ultimate hypocrite. After all the barroom debates and deep religious conversations, after years of looking down at followers and making fun of their "old man in the sky," after all the self-induced pats on the back, celebrating my intelligence and independence...in the end, I needed Him too.

THE SERVICE was finally over. It was time to pick up my son from the church-run daycare center.

On the way back to our car I saw something in the distance that stopped me in my tracks. Jim and Susie, the all-American couple who sat behind me, were now on a picnic bench outside in the school's courtyard. They were holding hands and crying.

WHAT ABOUT YOU?

1. Who/what has influenced you to search for God? How do you allow yourself to be challenged or engage in conversations with this person?

2. Do you think it is necessary to take care of all your personal issues before developing a relationship with God?

3. Do you see a need for God in your life right now? What impact would you like to see Him have on your life?

2

Gradually to Worship

She was walking out of the grocery store just as I was walking in. Our paths were on the verge of crossing when she started to speak to someone in the parking lot behind me saying, "Here comes Mommy! Mommy missed her little fellow. Yes she did!"

My feet instantly stopped all forward momentum and pivoted one hundred-eighty degrees. I am passive-aggressive by nature, but sometimes you just have to speak up. If this woman left a child in the car, on a warm summer day, then she deserved a piece of my mind.

The confrontation never happened. There was no need for it. As she approached her car, I could see "Mommy's little fellow" jumping up and down on the front seat. It wasn't a child. It was a Chihuahua.

Here's my point: dog people are weird!

Now, I love dogs, had one growing up. I will probably have one again someday. I'd pick a dog over a cat in a heartbeat and yet I have never talked to a dog like it's a person. To me that's just silly. People who do that—Dog People—are just a different breed.

What are you the most passionate about? Chances are, whatever it is, it's also the thing that makes you look a little ridiculous.

Do you have a friend who is really obsessive about a football team, either professional or college? Has he decorated a room, or perhaps the entire house with memorabilia? Has he named his first-born after his favorite player? Does he sit shirtless in an outdoor stadium in subzero degree temperatures with his chest painted green? Football is great, but these people are fools.

For the last several years I've lived in the South—in North Carolina and before that, Louisiana. Both states are havens for Civil War buffs. They recreate historic battles, turning them into major productions. A costume director hands out blue and gray uniforms. There's a prop department in charge of all the flags, tents, guns and cannons. They even have a special effects expert precisely timing explosions and a makeup artist creating missing limbs and other wounds. It all looks so real and authentic until you remember it's just a bunch of adults playing a big game of pretend—that can't be normal.

Nothing though, absolutely nothing, looks more bizarre to the outsider than how humans worship their God. Non-Catholics think the Rosary is strange. If you're not a Muslim or just geographically challenged, then praying in the direction of Mecca is totally confusing. And it's hard to believe your ears when you hear Charismatic Christians speaking in tongues. It all looks (and sounds) a little bit goofy, but each ritual, regardless of faith or denomination, is driven by passion.

I've thought a lot about my first visit back to church. Years have passed and a lot has changed since then, but one thing hasn't. My opinion on one issue has stayed the same. Those people with their hands up in the air singing praises to Jesus at the top of their lungs still freak me out. Do they know how crazy they look? I wonder if some of them are doing it just for show.

It's all kind of Biblical.

The book 2 Samuel records the story of the Ark of the Covenant returning to Jerusalem. For the Jews this actually meant that God would once again be living among them. That seems like enough reason to celebrate. King David (as in David and Goliath) was ecstatic that day—so happy that he starts dancing in the streets.

We don't know what style he used. It could have been the jig, the Moon Walk, the Tennessee Waltz, a clog, or the electric slide. Whatever it was, we know he looked ridiculous.

That's a fact because watching the spectacle from a distant window was David's wife Michal. The Bible actually uses the word "contempt." While she watched her husband prance around, "she was filled with contempt." Later in the same chapter she confronts David for all the embarrassment he has brought to the family, to the Kingdom and to all of Israel. Their marriage was never the same.

I thought about all this on a recent Sunday. The church band was playing one of my favorite songs. It's called *Mighty to Save.* Halfway through the tune is the line, "Now I surrender." When they got to that lyric my hand automatically, without any thought, went up in the air. Just like the people who freaked me out a few years earlier.

It's impossible to explain but it really was a moment of freedom. It had nothing to do with seeking attention. It wasn't: "Hey, look at me. I am a better Christian than you." It's kind of weird. Even though people were all around me, the act was very private; something I shared only with God. As my arm went up, it felt like it was lifting all the burdens off my shoulders and turning it over to him. It was very beautiful and special but it didn't last.

Turns out I am one part David and one very big part Michal.

The second my hand past my head and continued upwards, my mind kicked into gear. “Wow! What are you doing? Are you actually going to attempt the hand thing? No! No! No! Are you crazy? What are the people behind you going to think?”

It was up, it was down, within a blink of an eye. If the people behind me were thinking anything at all, it must have been “I think that guy just had a seizure! His arms are flapping all over the place!”

Even after all that has happened—which will unfold in the pages to come—I can still hear the voice of that skeptic sitting in his car in a middle school parking lot. He still has a hold on me. Consequently, religious worship too often remains all about the outside; how I look and come across to others.

What David understood, (heck, the dog woman, the football fan and the Civil War buff get this, too) is that when you are really passionate about something, when you really care about it—especially when it’s your relationship to God—then the only thing that truly matters is not the outside world, but what’s going on inside of you.

Part 2

The Hard Sell

"People who cover over their sins
will not prosper. But if they confess
and forsake them they will receive mercy."
(Proverbs 28:13 NLT)

"Anyone who claims to know all the answers
doesn't really know very much. But the person
who loves God is the one God knows and cares for."
(1 Corinthians 8:2-3 NLT)

3

The One That Got Away

If anyone gets the credit, or blame for that matter, for turning me into an Atheist, it has to be Amy Fowler. We only knew each other for a short period of time, a few months in high school, but the impact she had on my life lasted much longer.

She was gorgeous! Maybe one of the most beautiful women I've ever known. The image of her face has never left my mind. I nicknamed her "Chisel" because her features were flawless. A sculptor working in clay couldn't have carved out a more perfect vision.

The two of us attended different schools, but met through a mutual friend. An adolescent flirtation quickly started. Soon we were talking on the phone every night. "What kind of music do you like? What did you get on the SAT? What's your curfew? Would you like to go out Saturday night?"

"Ah.....well." She seemed a little confused and caught off guard. "Can you hold on a moment?"

When a woman puts down the receiver and walks away from the phone, just seconds after you asked her out, no matter how you cut it it's never a good sign. Amy's absence lasted for what seemed an eternity. "She's probably just being polite," I told myself. "Perhaps she is trying to cover up the sound of her laughter."

Suddenly the silence and the sweet feminine voice were replaced by a gruff, macho tone. "This is Mr. Fowler. I understand you want to date my daughter?"

I was totally thrown off my game. What was he doing on the phone? I was asking Amy to the movies, not for her hand in marriage! Clearly, there was a misunderstanding. I was about to straighten things out but the overprotective dad interrupted with a question.

"So Doug, what religion are you?"

"I'm Roman Cath..." The words were barely out of my mouth.

"I'm sorry," he rudely interrupted, "my daughter is not allowed to date Catholics."

CLICK!

HURDLE: THERE WAS CHRIST AND NOW THERE ARE CHRISTIANS

The problem with religion, any religion, is it becomes impossible to separate the faith from the followers.

In the last century a very unlikely source, a Hindu, provided incredible insight into Christianity. "I like your Christ," Mahatma Gandhi told a group of Western reporters. "He was completely innocent, offering himself as a sacrifice for the good of others, including his enemies, and became the ransom of the world. I like your Christ, but I do not like your Christians. If Christians would really live according to the teaching of Christ, as found in the Bible, all of India would be Christian today."

I, too, would have probably followed Christ much earlier, if only it weren't for the Christians who kept popping up in my life. Why was it that they always seemed far more interested in converting me than really getting to know me? Wasn't Christianity supposed to be about loving your neighbor? Why then, did their love seem to come with the condition that I first must think the way they do?

IN SPITE of her father's objections, Amy and I continued to talk virtually every night. The conversations were shorter and only took place during those hours when her father wasn't at home. As the kid brother of an older sister, I was well aware of what was going on. I had seen it firsthand in my own family. The parent's disapproval was actually working in my favor. Amy's dad had successfully turned me into forbidden fruit.

The tables were now turned. Amy was pursuing me, even asking me out. "Would you like to go to my church?" It was hardly the typical first date, but hey it was still a date....wasn't it?

The Fowler family were members of a Baptist church on the other end of the county. This would be the first Protestant service I had ever attended.

The sermon was on materialism. The pastor talked about the dangers of false idols. He questioned the faith of his congregation, especially those who openly bestowed praise on clothes, cars or houses. He concluded with a little fire and brimstone and told us if those objects continued to sever our relationship with God, we would pay the ultimate price: eternity in hell. "I want y'all to bow your heads and close your eyes."

He was on a roll now. "What if something happened on the way home tonight? I mean something horrible like a car wreck, is there anyone here who doesn't know if they'd go to heaven? If so, let me see your hands."

Certain moments in life cause you to take inventory. I may have only been a teenager, but my list of sins far outweighed my age. Even if my parents were in the dark, according to the Pastor, God was well aware of all I had done: gotten drunk, tried marijuana, cheated on tests, struggled with materialism (thinking I'd be more popular if only I had a cooler car or wardrobe) and okay, I was still a virgin, but that wasn't for a lack of trying.

"Maybe he's got a point," I thought to myself. "I guess if I were to die tonight I may not go to heaven." My hand slowly started to lift up in the air. It was barely above my shoulders when the preacher started screaming into the microphone, "Two people have their hands up! Come up! Come up you two and be saved by the Lord!"

Suddenly the entire congregation was on its feet singing *Amazing Grace*. The pastor wasn't exactly singing along. He was yelling the words, preaching the lyrics towards us heathens. "You were lost! But now you're found! You are blind, but come up and you will be able to see!"

To me it all seemed like a huge bait and switch. "No one said anything about being saved! What does that even mean?" My eyes were still closed. Both of my hands were now firmly down gripping the pew in front of me. Maybe if I held on tight enough I could stand my ground in spite of the mob mentality. "Two people? Just two people? How is that possible? There's got to be five hundred-plus here....the rest of them must be liars!"

"Come up and be saved!"

The preacher wasn't quitting. He was now announcing to the church that the other guy had made his way up front. "Welcome to the kingdom of Heaven, sir." The stranger's departure from my ranks only made me feel betrayed and even more isolated.

Perhaps, maybe, hopefully, was it at all possible that he didn't even see my hand? This is a huge room, it's not like I had it all the way up in the air. Anyway it was only up for a split second. Maybe he is talking about someone else.

"There is still someone out there. A young man sitting in the back…."

Dammit!

"We want you to come up! Be saved by the Lord!"

Suddenly, there was this overwhelming sense of a presence surrounding me. You ever have a moment in life when you know, without a doubt, that you are not alone? My eyes were shut but I could feel him, I could hear him, heck I could even smell him, "Is that Old Spice aftershave?" I opened my eyes and found a seventy-year old usher standing inches away from my face.

"You don't have to go up if you don't want to."

Within a second or two, the harassment stopped. The preacher said something about how the congregation "should keep that young man in your prayers." And with that we were dismissed.

Even with all the awkwardness, the date appeared to be successful. In the days following the church service, my flirtation with Amy reached an all-time high. She started to write notes, delivering them to me at school through our mutual friend. She even signed them with "XOXO."

Clearly, I was getting somewhere.

The following week she asked me out again. This time her youth group was having a kick ball game. Amy wanted me to play on her team.

After an uneventful game, the youth leader gathered all the teenagers together in a circle. We were instructed to hold hands and one-by-one we started to pray. Someone wanted to pray for a sick aunt, and then someone else said a prayer for the homeless and so forth and so on.

As the petitions to God bounced around the circle, I started to think about what I would say. Maybe I could use the opportunity to ask Amy out on a more formal date. What did I know about religious girls? Seemed to me you could really win one over by propositioning her in prayer. "Oh God, please let Amy go out with me this Saturday….and don't let her father find out."

I never got my chance. Amy went directly before me. She was standing to my right, holding my hand (but then we were all holding hands.) "Heavenly Father, I want to lift up all those who are not yet saved. Please let them understand your grace and mercy." Just as the words were leaving her mouth she started to squeeze my hand. It wasn't that squeeze that said, "Hey, you're kind of cute, Catholic Boy. Let's go out this weekend." It was more like; "Hey, I'm talking about you!"

Something about her words and that squeeze flicked a switch to a light bulb that revealed the first blemish on Chisel's face. All the hours on the phone, the notes she composed, all the flirtation…. I was just a project, just a mission. She didn't want me! She just wanted to convert me, to carve out another notch on her salvation bedpost.

Rejection is always hard to deal with and usually involves a complex string of emotions. Throw into the equation the fact that at the very moment the realization sunk in, that very split second, it was my turn to pray and you'll understand why things turned ugly.

"I'd just like to pray that…that…" I stopped and stammered and struggled to think of something profound to say, but in the end decided to go with what was genuinely in my heart. "I would just like to pray that the rest of the evening goes by very, very quickly!"

It actually turned out to be a rather long and painful night. The drive from the ball field to Amy's house was mile after mile of silence. When she got out of the car, we both probably knew that we would never see each other again, but neither of us bothered to say goodbye.

As she walked away, I was saddened by the way things turned out. Part of me was mourning the loss of this beautiful woman, but I was also thinking about the one that really got away that night. Deep down inside I knew my relationship with God, and certainly my involvement with religion, had come to an end.

Hurdle: A Fall From Grace

As a child of the 1980s, I grew up in a time when several high-profile Christians took very public falls from grace. In the second half of the decade, it was virtually impossible to turn on the television without hearing of some church scandal. Jim Baker went to jail for fraud, Jimmy Swaggart was caught with a prostitute—not once but twice!—and Oral Roberts got wrapped in controversy when he placed his life in the hands of loyal television viewers: "Send me eight million dollars or the Lord will call me home."

It wasn't just national figures. In my hometown everyone was talking about Father Nick. He showed up to church one Sunday with a black eye and busted lip. He told his stunned congregation that he had been the victim of a mugging, a rare crime for our suburban neighborhood. In reality, as revealed in a criminal warrant later, the wounds were the result of a drug deal gone bad. Perhaps more astonishing was that Father Nick wasn't using the drugs, he was selling them. When he went down, the local police claimed they had knocked the area's biggest drug king off his throne.

Watching all this as a child you just had to wonder: if followers are getting it so wrong, is what they're following also wrong?

DURING THE SUMMER BREAK following my first year in college, I was invited to a party thrown by an old high school buddy. It wasn't an official reunion, but virtually everyone from my class was there.

Standing in the corner of the kitchen, drinking a beer, was a familiar face. I instantly recognized the mutual friend who once introduced me to Chisel. I had known her for a long time. The two of us went back to the sixth grade. We needed to catch up. She went to college on a basketball scholarship, so we talked about the experience of her first season. We asked about each other's family and provided updates on our romantic life, which lead me to wonder: "What ever happened to Amy Fowler?"

"You haven't heard?" My friend's eyes instantly lit up. It was clear she had some good gossip to dish out. "She was kicked out of some very religious college in South Carolina. I think it's called Bob Jones University or something like that. Get a load of this: they kicked her out because she got pregnant! Yeah, someone knocked her up!"

Amy was not the first teenager I knew to have a baby out of wedlock. Three or four girls from my graduating class had already met the same fate. Some of these instances were not altogether a shock, but no one would ever have predicted that this would happen to Chisel.

Our mutual friend ended her news report with the typical cliché that someone says only after they've contributed to the rumor mill: "I need to call her up and see how she's doing."

Perhaps my friend's heart genuinely went out to Amy, but mine didn't. The scandal was like a personal victory. In a way, it kind of confirmed my decision not to believe in God. Suddenly, this noble and virtuous woman was written off as something far less than holy.

I wondered what her father thought about the ordeal. How much I wanted to call him up and gloat, "Sure, don't let her date Catholics. Well how are those Baptist boyfriends working out for you? What's that? I can't hear you, Grandpa!"

Confession: My Microscope Wasn't Very Fair

In today's world, Christianity has an image problem. It is plagued by the appearance of followers who are hypocritical, far too political, judgmental and intolerant of those who don't share their opinions.

The image problem exists because often times the charges are true. Many of the Christians I know have deserved one, if not all, of the labels above. And yet, to be honest with you, I deserved a few of those labels too. As a nonbeliever, I held myself up as an open-minded individual who accepted others no matter what their differences. My tolerance, though, only went so far. It did not extend to Christians.

I placed the believer under a microscope that specifically hunted for flaws, failings and shortcomings. Anytime my high-powered lens discovered an imperfection in character, I'd exploit the opportunity to question the sincerity of the believer's faith. "Clearly, if you were a REAL Christian, you wouldn't have done that!"

I justified my actions by claiming, "They asked for it." After all, they were the ones who set themselves apart. But now I wonder who really is to blame for that higher, at times unfair, standard. Is the problem with Christians trying to lift themselves above everyone else, or is the problem with a society that tries so hard to tear them down?

AT THE TIME of this writing, if I've done the math correctly, Amy's child would be either sixteen or seventeen years old. That's the same age we were when Chisel took me to church and tried to convert me.

It's impossible to think about those events without pondering how it all turned out in the end. Considering the circumstances and her upbringing, it is very likely that Amy carried the child to term, but I wonder if she kept it or gave it up for adoption.

What about Amy's dad? Did he disown her, kick her out of the house and turn his back on his daughter when perhaps she needed him the most? Of course, he also could have embraced this new addition to the family and become a loving grandparent helping Amy out both emotionally and financially.

And then there's the baby's father. Did he stay in the picture? Did he marry Amy? Did he provide child support? Did the little girl, or little boy, grow up knowing the love of their father? Or was Amy forced to be a single mom who had to figure out how to balance a baby, daycare bills, a full-time job, night school, rent, and all the while deal with the identity crisis that most people face in their early twenties?

More than a decade later, I, too would discover, in drastically different circumstances, just how difficult it is to raise a child as a single parent. It was during that time that my search for God started. I guess it just became clear that I couldn't do it on my own. Not many people can.

So mostly, these days, I wonder what happened to Amy's faith. Did the unplanned pregnancy bring her closer to God, driving her to her knees? Or did it push this once spiritual woman in the opposite direction? Did Amy's child grow up with the foundation of having a relationship with Christ, or was the concept of a higher power only something she heard about anytime she sneezed? *"God bless you."*

It took more than twenty years, but eventually God was getting around to answering my questions.

WHAT ABOUT YOU?

1. What is your view of believers? What has influenced that belief?

2. Have you ever taken pleasure in the failures of a Christian?

3. Do you know someone who has done something very un-Christian like, but whom you still respect as a believer? What causes you to maintain respect for him/her?

4

Gradually to Witnessing

I just turned off the computer, started packing things up, and was ready to go home. The work day was over. Actually, in terms of when I stopped getting paid, the day had ended a few hours earlier, but I stuck around to deal with things that seemingly couldn't wait until tomorrow.

Originally, at the start of the day, I had planned to go to the grocery store on my way home. The extra hours, though, had taken their toll. I had no desire to deal with the chaos of a supercenter. Besides, there was nothing on my list that seemed very urgent…wait a minute…yes there was. "I'm out of toilet paper!"

I work for a huge media conglomerate. It makes millions, if not hundreds of millions of dollars, every year. They're not going to fire me for stealing a roll of toilet paper. Come on, this is really no big deal. After all, I had just spent three hours working here off the clock. My unpaid service seemed like a pretty good trade off for what the company would lose in this white-collar crime.

And so I set out to commit grand theft T.P. It really wasn't a well-thought-out operation. I simply walked into the men's room, grabbed a roll and walked out…and then immediately bumped into a coworker.

He knew instantly what was going on. He looked at me, looked down at my hands, and saw one holding "the goods" and the other holding my briefcase. It was a clear getaway attempt. Embarrassment and fear overcame my body while my mind quickly rejected a number of possible excuses. "No! He'll never buy that."

The encounter with my coworker damaged my pride, but it was something else that really bothered me. He is a younger guy, a cool guy. There was no chance of him telling the boss. The real problem was, in the past few months he had started to attend my church on a regular basis.

Think about it. Is it possible that my act of crime could have foiled my coworker's faith? What if he wondered "Why am I going to church? Christians are all the same: liars, thieves, frauds and phonies." If that sounds far-fetched, isn't it basically what happened to me with Chisel?

And think about something else: What if he told other members of the congregation about my life of crime? No one there would ever look at me as the perfect Christian again.

In the book of Acts is the story of a married couple named Ananias and Sapphira. They were some of the earliest members of the faith. They lived in the days just following Jesus ascending into Heaven. During that time, Christians were part of a very close-knit community. Believers shared all their possessions and food. They sold their homes and property, contributing all of the proceeds to one fund. At least that is what they were supposed to do. Ananias and Sapphira did not. They gave a portion and kept the rest for themselves.

Church leaders confronted the husband first. Ananias lied to them. He claimed that his donation was the sum of the sale. As soon as the words were out of his mouth he falls to the ground, dead. A short time later his wife, who had yet to hear of her husband's passing, was confronted. Sapphira also lied about the donation and she, too, instantly dropped dead.

The story has nothing to do with money. It is not about how much you give to the church. Instead, it's about the divide between our words and our actions. It's about saying one thing and doing another. It's about the fragile attempt to maintain an image of someone who has it all together, living the perfect life, free of pain and drama...when in reality you're stealing toilet paper from work.

Somewhere along the way, maybe it was that day with Ananias and Sapphira, we created the myth that Christianity is all about getting things right. It's not. I think it's all about acknowledging when we get them wrong.

The morning after the "Great Paper Caper," the same coworker approached me. "I just want to ask you something. Did you covet the toilet paper before you stole it? I am just trying to figure out how many commandments you broke."

His joke made it clear that he understands Christianity better than I do. He knows that faith requires a certain level of vulnerability. You have to be willing to open up and expose not just the flaws and failings, but also the pain and suffering. Such revelations will not turn those weaknesses into a badge of honor, but it will do something far more important. They will remind people of why we need a savior in the first place.

Our shortcomings honestly tell a part of the Gospels that are too often misunderstood. Christ did not die on the cross for our sins because He thought we would get it right. Instead, He knew one day a college girl would fall into temptation and get pregnant. He knew that believers would lie about their finances. And yes, maybe He also knew that a self proclaimed "born-again Christian" would be caught stealing work supplies. You see, the true beauty of the cross, what really needs to be our message, is that Christ died for our sins knowing how much we would get it wrong.

Only when we're willing to be authentic will we truly see how powerful a light we can be to others. But then again, I am hardly objective on this topic. My views are tainted by the memory of a young couple crying on a picnic table.

PART 3

SORROW

"Sorrow is better than laughter,
for sadness has a refining influence on us."
(Ecclesiastes 7:3)

"We can rejoice, too, when we run into
problems and trials, for we know that they
are good for us—they help us learn to endure."
(Romans 5:3)

5

THE JOY OF PAIN

The image of Jim and Susie haunts me. I can still see them sitting on the picnic table, Susie covering her face with her left hand, her shoulders shaking from the painful expression of emotion. Jim holding her right hand, trying to comfort her while brushing back tears of his own.

What was bothering them? It had to be something big. Was it cancer or an illness? Maybe Jim was having an affair. Maybe Susie had suffered a miscarriage. One of them could have lost a job. The home could be under foreclosure. Heck, Jim could even be facing a potential indictment on murder charges and looking at a life sentence in a federal prison. Okay, that one is a stretch, but I wasn't about to rule anything out.

The contrast was so confusing. An hour earlier these same two people appeared to have it all. They were the "all-American" couple singing praises to their God without a worry in the world. And now look at them! They were almost unrecognizable.

It sounds horrible, but I liked this Jim and Susie far more than the earlier version. Somehow through their tears and pain they appeared more real, more tangible, more human and most importantly, more like me.

When you're suffering, as I was that day, you need to know that you're not alone. That somewhere out there, someone is hurting as much as you. My life was falling apart, and it seemed like no one else understood. And yet they did. At least Jim and Susie did.

The more I thought about the contrast, the more it all seemed to make sense. The sudden transformation of these two people served as another reminder of how quickly life can change. One day things are going your way, and the next day they're not.

Looking at Jim and Susie, I couldn't help but wonder when exactly my life fell off the tracks.

HURDLE: THE PRICKLE-LY PERCH

Where have all the milestones gone?

At the start of life, things are always moving. We go from one accomplishment to another. Even as an achievement is celebrated our eyes are already focused on the next thing to be conquered. A child is born; one day he rolls over, sits up, starts crawling, walking, and then in the blink of an eye it's a kindergarten graduation. Brownies turn into Girl Scouts, Cub Scouts turn into Boy Scouts, a tricycle turns into a set of training wheels leading to the ultimate day when they can be removed, high school turns into college, college turns into a first job, the first job turns into middle management…and then everything suddenly comes to a screeching stop.

"What gives here? I was going places. Things were happening for me. I was the whiz kid. Everyone talked about all

my great potential. Now it feels like I am stuck in neutral. Is this all there is to life? What is all this about anyway?"

Hitting the snag is so common that author Theodor Geisel (Dr. Seuss) wrote about it in his bestselling book: The Places You'll Go. He had a special name for that moment when everything slows down. He called it the "Prickle-ly Perch, caught in a lurch."

"You'll come down from that Lurch with an unpleasant bump.
And the chances are, then, that you'll be in a Slump.
When you're in a Slump, you're not in for much fun.
Un-slumping yourself is not easily done."

EVERYONE AROUND ME probably knew I was going through a crisis. If they had any doubt, all they had to do was look at my hair. It was changing colors on a daily basis. My normally dark brown, anchorman-style had turned completely gray overnight. The next day there was a tint of blue, followed by a green hue and finally my head was canary yellow.

The phenomenon was caused by some really bad advice from my agent and a career that was going nowhere.

Not long before, things had been like clockwork, going along just as I had planned. Life was easy. It was just a matter of being ambitious, determined, and never giving up. After college, I got a job anchoring the news in a small television market and very quickly moved to one bigger city after another. One day, a third-place station in Albuquerque called looking for me to be their savior. They needed a high-profile investigative reporter to knock down doors and solve viewer problems. They were going to name the entire station after my work. "Doug Wahl and News 13 are On Your Side!"

It didn't work. Two years into the experiment the ratings hadn't budged and the station decided to go in another direction, without me. Oh, I still had a job. There was still a year left on my contract, but there was really nothing for me to do. No place for me to contribute. My daily routine became plugging the holes left vacant by those out sick or on vacation. It felt like my purpose in life was suddenly gone.

"Doug, let's face it. You're not exactly a Ken doll." Agents don't pull punches. They like to knock you down before they lift you up. "All I am saying is we're not going to get you a job on your looks. Let's try the distinguished approach. Maybe you should dye your hair gray."

My agent knew nothing about cosmetology. As it turns out, you really can't dye your hair gray. Instead they bleach it blond and try to add the gray on top of that. The problem starts once you wash your hair. The gray rinses away, leaving the blue, the green and the eventual canary yellow. In the end, instead of that distinguished newscaster look, I more resembled a punk rocker with an addiction to meth. Turns out, there's not a big demand for that style in the television industry.

Looking back it all seems kind of funny, but at the time it felt like the world was coming to an end. The change of job and loss of purpose really did bring on a deep depression. It lasted for several months, maybe even longer. During that time there was just nothing to be hopeful about. The future seemed totally bleak.

What do people do when they're down? They cling to anything that provides a moment of happiness. For me that included hanging out at the same watering hole every night, gambling at casinos and chasing women.

One night this amazingly beautiful woman walked by my table at the bar. She was so pretty that I instantly did a double take. My head snapped back around just to catch a second glimpse, which was even better than the first. I had no chance with a woman like that. What would she see in a twenty-nine-year-old with a head of gray hair and no hopes for the future?

It was a kamikaze mission, but nonetheless I was getting up from the table to go and introduce myself.

Hurdle: The Fault, Dear Brutus...

His divorce took place at least twenty years ago, but to hear him talk you'd think it happened last week.

"I knew she was cheating on me."

The breakup is still one of his favorite topics. Sometimes I think my friend is incapable of discussing anything else.

"Did I tell you how she emptied the bank account before leaving me? She took everything!"

There is a lot of truth to what he says. I've met the ex-wife and have no problem believing his stories. And yet something bothers me. Even if his version is a hundred percent accurate (and of course it's not), even if he was a loving and supportive husband, even if he was the victim, even if she cheated on him, even if she was the one who decided to leave, most of the blame still belongs on his shoulders. That is because regardless of what she did to him, he is the one who decided to keep the pain and the bitterness a part of his life for the last two decades.

I think he chose that path because in a weird way it was the easiest of two options. The other choice requires a toughness he lacks. The pain of his past is like a heavy rock tied around his ankle. He's mastered the art of dragging it along wherever he goes, but he needs to be stronger still to lift up the rock and face all the ugliness hidden underneath.

I could tell the story of the romance with that woman from the bar in a couple of ways. And both, as far as the facts are concerned, would be true.

One version would focus on how badly I got the shaft. You'd feel sorry for me. I could tell you that I gave up my broadcasting dreams to follow her from New Mexico to Louisiana. You might be ashamed to know that we moved in with each other, but perhaps proud to learn that I got a responsible job in management and financially supported her. I could talk of becoming a dad, and how after our son was born, my life slowed down while she continued to party. You may ask why I gave her a second chance when the other man came along, and I am not sure I could answer that…nor could I make sense of how hard I tried to keep our family together when the man after that, a friend of mine, came along too.

The same story could also be told by focusing on my role in the troubled relationship. This would require me to reveal unflattering and embarrassing details, but the simple fact that I was admitting them would make me sound honorable. Maybe I should have given her access to my bank account. Heck, we were already living together, acting like husband and wife. Giving her control of the money wouldn't have been that much of a stretch. I should have been nicer to her friends; they thought I looked down on them, and I did. Too often she was put in a position to choose between me and them. It probably would have been wise to cut ties with my old girlfriends, especially that one she really didn't like. It never seemed like a big deal. The woman lives in another state. But now, looking back, I know cheating isn't just a physical issue, it can also be done emotionally, too.

Each version is based on facts, but neither one is totally accurate. Truth is seldom an issue of what was said or done. In the end it almost always comes down to the motive.

You see, the events and the words really don't matter because our relationship was doomed from the start. When we met, my life was in such upheaval that all I wanted was to win acceptance from anyone or anything—from another television station offering a job, from the laughter of the drunk next to me at the bar, from the perfect combination of dice on the craps table and especially (most importantly of all) from a beautiful woman. From day one, our romance was built on a foundation of receiving love, not giving it.

That insight should have made the breakup easier, but it didn't. Because there was a child involved, it actually made things worse. A little boy would pay the price for my fears and insecurities by growing up in a broken home. That's really why I wanted our family to stay together. I just didn't have what it takes to sacrifice my son.

Confession: I Didn't Believe in God, But I was Still Mad at Him

If you're courting someone of the opposite sex, your strategy is probably to flatter them. The better the object of your affection feels in your presence, the more time she'll want to spend with you. So you send roses, open car doors, and constantly tell her "You're beautiful."

God builds relationships, at least with some of us, using a totally different approach. He wants to prove that He is the only one we need, but to do that sometimes He has to become the only one we've got.

IF LOSING MY JOB led me into a depression, then losing my family lead me into a fit of rage. I was mad at the world and everyone in it.

I hated my ex for throwing our son's childhood away. I hated the most recent "other man" for stabbing me in the back. I hated myself because ultimately I should have known better. And most of all I hated God. Oh, I didn't believe in Him, but at that moment I just couldn't shoulder all of the blame.

It's really strange. All at once the events of my life were pushing and pulling me in opposite directions. On the one hand, the breakup seemed like further proof that no higher power existed. "A loving God would not have done this to me." And yet I had to admit that by making this supernatural figure the recipient of my anger and hatred, I was at the same time acknowledging Him.

If only I had been more aware of the Bible, perhaps I would have realized that pain is one of God's favorite tools. He uses it all the time to build faith. Isn't that what he did with Lazarus?

WHAT ABOUT YOU?

1. Have you reached the point when you wonder: "What is life all about?"

2. What role did you play in the problems that are currently plaguing your life?

3. Have you ever been mad at God? What caused it? What was the outcome?

6

GRADUALLY TO HEALING

"Guys, I've got something to tell you."

My friend is the macho type, the kind of man who rarely shows emotion. Still it was clear that something was horribly wrong.

"I should have told you all a long time ago, but the right moment never came up."

He was addressing a group of guys who meet once a week. It's a strange gathering of Christian men. We're a cross between a Bible study and a poker night.

"About fifteen years ago," my friend continued, "I was diagnosed with AIDS."

It was a startling revelation, but none of us were altogether shocked. Our friend has been very open about his past. He is a reformed womanizer. His first marriage ended after an affair. He met his second wife at a strip club. That union didn't last long either.

"I have to take these medications every day." Our friend was pulling bottle after bottle out of a plastic bag. He was telling us how this cocktail of drugs had kept the disease at bay. "But I don't know what I am going to do now. The insurance company isn't going to cover the prescriptions anymore. It's going to cost at least $2,000 a month! I don't have that kind of money!"

The hardest part about coming to Christ later in life is that you never feel like you totally escape your past. It is always there. Always lingering, always lurking around the corner. My friend understands: "I don't get it. It was my fault that I got AIDS. I made a lot of mistakes back then. But what have I done wrong now? All this time I've been trying to be a man of God. I've been going to church, tithing, praying every night. Why would He do this to me now? What have I done to deserve this?"

Lazarus being raised from the dead is one of the most famous stories in the Bible. The first time you read it you sit back and say, "Wow! If Jesus really brought a man back from the grave, He must be the son of God." And yet I don't think that is the most important fact in the story.

Read it a few more times and you'll see that the scripture is not so much about Jesus doing something amazing as it is about him doing nothing at all.

Look what happens when He first learns that His friend is ill. There's no concern. He doesn't rush to Lazarus' bedside; He just sits still. He doesn't move for two days. By the time He does it is too late. His friend is already dead. Lazarus' sisters are already in mourning. One even comes close to blaming Jesus for not arriving earlier: "If only you had been here my brother would not have died."

It all, of course, works out in the end when Jesus performs a miracle that greatly increases the faith of His followers. It makes sense: Lazarus needed to die before Jesus could bring him back to life.

As dramatic as the ending is, somehow it gets in the way of a very important point: for this event to play out, real human pain was necessary. People had to suffer before something great could happen. Someone had to endure an illness and lose his life. Others had to be left in tears in a total state of despair. I wonder if in their grief, either of the sisters asked the same question of my friend: "What have we done to deserve this?"

Before my friend could finish telling his story, he was interrupted. The man who politely took over the floor was a virtual stranger. He was our newest member. This may have been the first time he ever spoke up. He didn't need to say much before once again it was clear that something was horribly wrong. "I haven't told this to anyone, not even my parents. A few weeks ago I was diagnosed HIV positive."

The confession of the second friend did nothing to end the problems of the first. Yes, in time his insurance would come back, but he still had to endure months of red tape, a rationed supply of medication, and a personal budget crisis. Still, from the moment the second revelation was spoken, his struggles had found purpose. What was happening to him was no longer about him. He was able to become absorbed in someone else's worries. Even though both friends were struggling, one became a mentor to the other.

When things go wrong, we spend far too much time wondering why. No doubt, I did that with Jim and Susie. I so desperately wanted to know the reason behind their tears. In the end the reason didn't matter. Perhaps I should have paid more attention to the results.

The result of a man suffering and dying was that a handful of others had the required faith to form a church. The result of a friend losing his insurance was that another friend would not be forced to go through a crisis alone. The result of two strangers crying on a picnic table is that I no longer felt like that much of an outsider.

The following week I showed up at the middle school again.

PART 4

RELATIONSHIP

"The Lord said to me, 'You are my son.
Today I have become your father.'"
(Psalm 2-7)

7

FATHERS AND SONS

This is an intermission of sorts. When the first version of this book was completed, it did not include this chapter. The manuscript didn't need it. It was designed to help nonbelievers who wanted to believe. It took people through my spiritual journey and gave them tips on how they too could make the transformation from Atheist to Christian.

Like many new believers, I was excited to share my faith and wanted to help people build a relationship with God. So I printed copies on regular letter-sized paper, then placed them in binders and gave them away. All people had to do was read what I had written and tell me how much my words inspired their life.

It didn't exactly happen that way.

"Doesn't make sense," said a longtime friend. "Something is missing. In the first half you're an Atheist and then suddenly you're a Christian. What brought on the change? How did it happen? I just don't get it!"

There seems to be a general assumption that any life-changing transformation must be caused by a major event. In a way, the Bible supports this theory. It writes of Saul, a devoted Jew who hunts down and kills Christians until one day he is knocked off his horse by a flash of light. The event completely changes him. He even gets a new name. Saul becomes Paul, the man who would go on to write much of the New Testament.

Even if they're not believers, people can understand the concept of a spiritual cause and effect. They get a guy being struck by lightning (or whatever it was that hit Saul) and then becoming a new person. They've seen it in their own lives. They know former drug addicts who are now major Bible thumpers because of some vision. They've heard the testimony of a church volunteer who not too long ago suffered from severe depression and planned on ending it all, only to hear a voice that told him things would get better. And they have example after example of co-workers, neighbors, relatives and acquaintances who prayed for a miracle. They may doubt that miracle actually happened, but they know their friend believes it did and that is good enough for them.

The problem is my journey doesn't have such a dramatic event. Oh, there was this one moment that was very special (I write about it in the next chapter), but looking back it really wasn't the story of my conversion. Instead it was more like the instant I *realized* that I was converted. I didn't so much become a Christian as much as I kind of grew into the role.

How do you explain that to someone who doesn't share your faith? Heck, explaining it to some Christians is tricky. They too often demand a "flash of light" or "born again" moment. But that is not how it happened for me.

I'll admit that it seems like something is missing. Then again, maybe it's a little bit like becoming a parent.

HURDLE: GAME PLAN

I am a big believer in game plans. Every major transition in my life has been made only after designing a blueprint.

There was a game plan when I moved from reporting into management. It detailed how my new career would grow and foster. But in the end, nothing went according to the timetable.

Years later, when I started to dream about forming my own company, I wrote a business plan on paper. The move would be made when there was a certain amount of money in the bank account, when investors were on board, when the stars and the moon lined up perfectly. Eventually I did quit my job, and pursued my goals even though none of the prerequisites had been met.

The journey to faith started with a similar strategy. It called for me to become a believer once all my questions were answered and all the doubt had been erased. That still hasn't happened, but somehow I managed to become Christian anyway.

One life change, above all others, was in total and complete violation of its corresponding game plan. Strangely enough, the transition started with the sign of a cross. Well, okay, that may be a stretch, but at least a plus sign is close to the shape of a cross.

IT DOESN'T TAKE LONG to get the results of a home pregnancy test. You put the little strip into the plastic cup and within moments you know the answer. And yet, if the potential new addition to the family isn't a wanted blessing, then that brief period of time feels like forever.

I always wanted to be a father, but not like this. As I waited for the results, nothing about my situation seemed right.

What happened to all my plans to see the world? There were so many places I wanted to visit, so many cultures I wanted to absorb. The plan was to get my passport filled up before children came along. After all, you really can't travel with kids.

My career wasn't where it was supposed to be either. Now that I was in management, my focus needed to be on climbing the corporate ladder. A child coming into the world at this time could only slow down my progress.

Money was a problem too. There wasn't enough of it, at least not enough for me and a baby. Right now, after the bills were paid, there were always a few extra dollars left over to play golf or go to a nice restaurant. If that test came out positive, all the stuff I did for myself would come to an end. Wouldn't it be so much better if parenthood waited for my salary to increase?

Most of all, my concerns were about the relationship. A child should be born to two parents who love each other, who don't bicker and fight. That wasn't the case here. We had a lot of great times, but with each passing week the differences between us were coming to the surface. This was not the woman who was supposed to bear my child. It would be so much better if I waited for the right one to come along.

All of these issues were really conditions. My mind had a clear vision of how things should work out. If only I had planned differently, made some other decisions in life, perhaps things would have been more in line. For now, everything was out of my hands.

Time's up!

I turned to my girlfriend to see if she was ready to get the results. To my surprise, in the few moments it took for the strip to change colors, she had fallen asleep in a family room chair.

Alone, I walked into the bathroom. I didn't even need to pick up the cup. The plus sign was clear from across the room. Like it or not, I was about to go down a path filled with even more road blocks.

HURDLE: IT'S NOT ABOUT ANSWERS, IT'S ABOUT A RELATIONSHIP

My spiritual mentor is a guy by the name of Richie. His story is similar to mine. He started attending church only after problems erupted in his marriage. He approached faith with many of the same intellectual questions and emotional issues that I had. In spite of it all, not only did he become a Christian, he eventually quit his high-paying job as a beer distributor and joined the church staff.

It never appeared that Richie was driven by the need to convert me. His faith seemed far more secure than that, his friendship far more genuine. I really think he actually cared for me as a person, regardless of whether I thought or acted the way he did. He never preached the Gospel to me; he lived it.

What's strange, looking back on all our long conversations, is that my new friend never really answered any of my questions. Instead, Richie would always respond to one of my big religious concerns with the same sentence: "Yep, I used to struggle with that too."

It was nice to know that someone really understood where I was coming from, but after a while that response started to annoy me. I felt like Richie was holding out. "What does that mean, 'used to?' How did you get past it? How did you move on?"

For the first time, Richie didn't dismiss the question. Instead he answered it with words that totally confused me. "You never get past it. Most of the things you wonder about never get answered. You just get to a point when they really don't matter anymore. You get to a place where figuring things out is no longer all that important."

WHEN DID I BECOME A FATHER? That's a strange question. The answer ought to be obvious, but it's not. Oh, I know that legally it happened on September 10th at 10:21 a.m. While it was a great moment, and yes I instantly fell in love with him, the birth of my son was not the pivotal event in my road to fatherhood.

That day was just way too chaotic. He came into this world by means of a Cesarean delivery. Consequently the operating room was filled with doctors, nurses, machines that were beeping and buzzing, and the strange smell of burning flesh. In a waiting room outside was everyone my girlfriend had ever met: mother, father, aunts, uncles, cousins, high school friends and co-workers. All of them wanted to see this little boy, to hold him, to kiss him. It wasn't long before they probably spent more time with him than I did.

It wasn't until sometime after we got home that I really became a father, but even then the exact moment remains a mystery. Perhaps it was the first middle-of-the-night feeding, when it was just the two of us awake, bonding with each other. Maybe it happened when I took him outside and showed him his first tree, cloud and butterfly. Early on I learned how to make him laugh and giggle; perhaps goofing around with him is when the transition happened.

Clearly it had already taken place by that one special day. He was only a few months old. His mom was holding him, trying to get him to stop crying, but nothing she did worked. Finally, in frustration, she handed him to me. The instant he moved into my arms, the tears and the noise stopped. He simply wanted to be with his dad.

In that moment, none of the conditions I had placed on fatherhood had gone away. But none of them mattered anymore. My son didn't care how many countries I had visited or how much money was in my bank account, or where I was located on the career ladder. In the coming years he would know some of the problems between his mother and father, but at that moment, even that wasn't an issue for him.

If I could go back and re-live a portion of my life, I would return to those few minutes when an infant's tears subsided and turned to another bout of laughter and giggling. It was a great moment, but even still it is not when I became a father. It's just when I realized that the transformation had already taken place.

You see, I can't tell you the exact moment when I became a dad or a Christian. But I know that reaching both destinations had a lot in common. In time, each became less and less about a theory, or list of conditions, and more about a relationship. The journey to fatherhood and faith both required the same step on my part. To arrive at either, I first had to get to know the son.

CONFESSION: I STILL SEARCH FOR THE MOMENTS

When Christians speak of their faith, often times, they only tell part of the story. Perhaps for obvious reasons they choose to focus on those moments when God's presence proved overwhelming in their lives, so they talk of prayers that were answered overnight, scripture that leaped off the pages and spoke directly to them, and an undeniable feeling of love that was so powerful and warm that it actually changed them.

What they rarely tell you is that sometimes, more often than we care to admit, God seems very distant. Our prayers are interrupted with thoughts of work or the grocery list. You read the Bible only to see words on paper with no apparent application to your life. You ask for wisdom and guidance but in return only hear a long and painful silence.

Who's to blame for the separation? Perhaps the fault is ours. If we're honest, maybe we can admit that the pursuit of that feeling sometimes gets in the way of our worship of God.

AFTER THE BREAKUP, in the first days of our joint-custody agreement, the time I spent with my son was intentionally filled with major events. We were always on the go: to the playground, to the movies, to the beach, to the pool, to the fun zone, to the museum, to the circus. Perhaps it was my competitive nature, but more likely it was my insecurity. I wanted to be the cool parent. If going to Dad's house for the week was an adventure, then maybe my son would love me a little bit more.

You want to know the truth? It took me a long time to realize this, but the most precious and sweetest memories, when my son did something cute or said something funny, almost always came out of mundane and ordinary situations: brushing his teeth, taking a bath, getting sick, performing a puppet show, listening to a bedtime story.

You see, as a father, and as a follower, I want so much to feel that love, to bask in that warmth, that sometimes I try to create a special moment and almost completely overlook the ones that happen all on their own.

WHAT ABOUT YOU?

1. How would you describe the birth of your faith, in an instant or more of a process? Explain.

2. If you could have the answer to one spiritual question what would it be? If you never got the answer to that question, would you still be able to choose a relationship with God?

3. Describe a moment when you were overwhelmed with the presence of God. How often do those moments happen? What is your response when he seems distant?

8

GRADUALLY TO GOD

Randy goes to church every Sunday. He's joined a small group. He's recently started to pray with his wife. He knows all about Jesus and believes that Christ died on the cross for his sins. He even wears a crucifix around his neck. And yet Randy is not sure that he's really a Christian.

His confession shocked me. You see a guy at church, walking around with a Bible, and you just come to the conclusion that he's a Christian. How is it possible that this man of faith could doubt where he stands? The answer became clear when our recent lunch conversation turned to the topic of baptism.

"I want to do it," Randy told me, "but I just don't know what I'd say in the video."

Our church films a formal sit-down interview with each person who gets baptized. The testimonials are broadcast in front of the entire congregation on Sunday morning. The moment the interview ends, after you hear what Jesus means to that individual, a light shines on the corner of the stage where a small pool has been constructed. That person gets dunked, everyone applauds and someone hits play on the next story.

"What am I going to say? What am I going to tell people?"

It was clear that the issue weighed heavily on Randy's heart. "I've never had a drug or alcohol problem. My marriage has never been in serious trouble. My kids have always been in good health. What are people going to get out of my story? What am I going to tell them that Jesus saved me from?"

It was clear what Randy needed: a guy's trip to Vegas. You know, take a long weekend off and pack in as much sin as possible. It's an important cause. Randy's testimony needs a little more sex appeal. I could help with that. What are friends for? The two of us could bet away his mortgage. I'll even pick out the showgirl to destroy his marriage. And as God as my witness, his cocktail glass will never go empty. If I do my job right, as his friend and as a Christian brother, by the time we fly back Randy's life will be in shambles. When he finally sobered up, he would have the perfect story to tell in the interview.

All kidding aside, I think a lot of people suffer from the same problem that plagues Randy. Call it the "Good Guy Syndrome." Growing up, he probably had some foundation of faith. Maybe his parents specifically talked about God and Jesus, or perhaps they just taught their son to be mindful of other people's feelings. Randy took those lessons to heart and truly spent his life trying to care for those around him. And now, because of the good decisions he's made, it's become hard for him to take the next step.

"For God so loved the world that he sent his only Son, so that everyone who believes in Him will not perish but have eternal life." John 3:16 is arguably the most famous verse in the New Testament. You've seen it posted on signs at sports events, and for many Christians it's the first line they memorize by heart. The words matter to me not so much because of what was said, but because of who heard them. In that line of scripture Jesus was talking to a guy named Nicodemus.

If the Bible records the exact moment when Saul becomes Paul, it totally leaves us hanging on the transformation of Nicodemus. We know he was basically a good guy, an intelligent man who was sincere about his faith, but he had questions: "What do you mean 'born again?' Does one have to return to his mother's womb?"

Nicodemus makes two more cameo appearances in the Bible. Perhaps he became a follower in the middle of the book of John, when he stands up to other Jewish leaders who are plotting to arrest Jesus. Clearly there is a change. We know that he must be a believer after the crucifixion. That's when this man of great doubt, with so many good questions, risks his own life to make sure that Jesus is given a proper burial.

Where's the lightening strike and the falling off the horse? Where's the sound of God's voice coming from a burning bush? Where's the trip to Vegas? How did he become a believer in the absence of something major? Doesn't the story of Nicodemus lack a lot of pizzazz?

There's a saying at my church that if you invite a friend just once, then God will give them a nugget to keep coming back. It's true of Randy. In fact he recently started volunteering on the production staff, ironically helping to shoot, edit and produce the very videos that frighten him so much.

And still I worry far more about him than any of my friends who stay away on Sunday morning. He is still seeking, still searching, still scrambling to find that allusive piece of the puzzle. Without it his faith will always lack conviction.

Who's to blame? Perhaps not really him. Randy is just part of a larger church culture that continues to put emphasis on the most dramatic stories of conversion. Salvation is just more tangible when there's a moment in time that moves an individual from bad to good or from old to new.

But the root of those stories is really no different than those whose journey may appear tame, or even boring, in comparison. So does it matter if they're a Paul moving from absolute darkness into the light or a Nicodemus where the transformation is more gradual, sometimes lost in the contrast of white on white? In either case, the central figure remains someone who starts out living a life separate from their Lord and Savior.

I will continue to pray for my friend Randy. I will ask that God grants him the moment he is so desperately seeking. But perhaps, like me, it will only happen in hindsight.

PART 5

ACCEPTANCE

"If you try and keep your life for
yourself, you will lose it. But if you give
up your life for me, you will find true life."
(Matthew 16:25 NLT)

9

A Pink Sheet of Paper

I hate business conferences. It doesn't matter what you call them: retreats, seminars, forums, conventions, they're all the same. They always take place in some drab, windowless banquet center. Aspiring professionals work the room looking to further their careers, make connections, network, and distribute resumes and business cards. Some people love this type of thing. To me the business conference is an extreme waste of time.

It either centers around one speaker and his dreadfully boring slide show or facilitator who likes to break up the crowd, into smaller groups to play some kind of survival game. "Let's all pretend that we were on a bus that got stranded in the woods during a snow storm." The people around me start debating whether they should stay on the bus or go looking for help. Meanwhile, I spend my time trying to figure out which of my teammates I'd eat first. I almost always select the person who seems to be enjoying the assignment the most. It seems to me that anyone who can be so enthusiastic at a business conference, is the last person you actually want to be stuck with in a blizzard.

Once, not long after starting to go back to church, I got stuck at a retreat in Emerald Isle, North Carolina.

My attendance at this particular seminar was required by my boss. He forced me to go. He sent me alone. I wouldn't even be mingling with people in my own industry; instead I would have to endure the small talk of local business leaders and politicians. To make matters worse, this wasn't just a one-time affair. The two-day getaway was part of a getting-to-know you session for a committee of people who would have to meet once a month for the next year.

"Let's break the ice by doing a little project." Our group leader was a soft-spoken former social worker who looked like he couldn't quite let go of the 1960s. "Fold this pink sheet of legal paper into fours. In one box I want everyone to draw a picture, no words, just a picture of something that was important to you when you were ten years old. In the next box draw something that was important to you ten years ago. In box number three I want to see something that is important to you today. And finally, in the last box, draw something that will be important to you ten years into the future."

It was a ridiculous assignment, a total waste of time. We're a group of grown adults. So why are we being forced to do arts and crafts followed by the inevitable show and tell? How in the world did I get roped into an entire year of this crap?

And yet, as I hate to admit it, that pink sheet of legal paper helped change my life.

HURDLE: THE FUTURE WITH GOD

The best advice ever given to me came from the scariest man I ever met. Mr. Tank was a military man, a Captain in the Navy, who lived next door to my parents. He treated me, and all the other neighborhood kids, like we were enlisted men.

Venturing outside, especially on a summer evening, always came with the risk of bumping into Mr. Tank. He usually could be found on his front porch with a Scotch in one hand and an unfiltered cigarette in the other. If he caught you on his first drink you might escape with just a "hello." If it was his second or third, chances are he would try to engage you in a conversation. More likely he'd give you a lecture or maybe even try to recruit you into the service.

After trapping me on one particular night, he dropped a bombshell in my lap that has stayed with me ever since. "Life is pretty simple, Doug. All you got to do is figure out what's the most important thing. After that, everything else becomes either an asset or a liability."

Those words became my mantra. Once you establish a goal the rest becomes rather simple. Other opportunities and decisions will either move you closer to what you want to accomplish or pull you farther away.

Mr. Tank's advice was vital. His words helped me make it through college and get my career off the ground. But there is something he didn't tell me, something that I wasn't prepared for. Sometimes, the most important thing in your life changes.

THE FIRST BOX on the pink sheet of legal paper was easy to figure out. My hand instantly started drawing a ball and a bat. To a ten-year-old there is nothing more important than baseball. The sport holds meaning because of those special Little League memories, but it's more than that. In many ways baseball helps define a boy's relationship with his father. The two play catch together in the backyard. The father buys the son his first pack of trading cards. If they're lucky, they live close enough to a big league park to attend a few games. If not, they watch the World Series together on television. Virtually all the men in the group put baseball in the first box.

Everyone also mentioned their career. This was, after all, a group of business and community leaders. We varied on the icon used to depict our job and the box we placed it in, but work was important to all of us. The youngest in our gathering drew their careers under the "now" category. To me, it was more along the lines of what was important ten years ago. So in box number two I drew a picture of a television microphone and camera.

The third box belonged to my son. I'm not much of an artist. The stick figure really didn't do him justice. "You can't tell from this picture," I told the group when it was my time to present. "He really is the most handsome boy in North America."

The future box gave me the most trouble. Funny, because there was a time when I had the future all figured out. But recently so much unforeseen had taken place in the present that the future was a complete mystery. Initially I wanted to place my son again in the fourth box, but I didn't think they would let me get away with using the same answer twice.

And so I started to think about the only other thing that was making me feel good in my life, the only other thing that seemed to make sense. I thought about the last few months of attending church and what that meant to me. I thought about the friends I had met. They were not the typical Christians; they were people who I really wanted in my life. Most of all, I thought about this inner peace that was developing inside of me. Very little about my circumstances had changed. The breakup was still official. I was still separated half the time from my son,

I was still a grown man living in a shoebox-sized apartment meant for a college student, and yet—in spite of it all—as I stared at the pink sheet of paper, something inside of me told me everything would be okay.

I still had spiritual doubts, still had religious questions. They didn't just go away or magically disappear. At the same time, the truth is, a number of my issues were resolved. I now believed that Jesus was a real historic figure. I wasn't sure before. When you considered the brutal way in which He died, for me it was inhumane to continue to dismiss Him as a con artist or a swindler. People who are trying to pull "a fast one" don't willingly endure that kind of torture. At the very least I had to acknowledge that Jesus believed that He was who he claimed to be. When I learned that all but one of His Apostles were killed in a similar horrific fashion, it became clear to me that they must have seen something real, something worth losing their lives over.

It's funny, in that moment the concept of a God was still hard for me to accept, but somehow I worked my way around Him and arrived at a point where I truly believed in His son. Because of that, there was absolute faith on what belonged in the final box. My hand started to draw a winding road that faded off the edge of the paper. "I didn't know how else to symbolize it," I told the group, "but I recently started my walk and I am very excited to see where that will take me in the next ten years."

HURDLE: ON THE ROAD TO SALVATION

Too many believers reduce salvation to a prayer. Their approach seems to be:"If you want to get into heaven, then say these words and repeat after me." It's not that salvation is more complicated than reciting a sentence or two; actually I think it is simpler than that.

Say, for instance, the friend you invite to church decides to answer the altar call. The sermon really hits home. It was like something on the inside was telling him he was supposed to be here today. For the first time he really understands the meaning of the Cross. Suddenly it all makes sense: people are born with a sinful nature and God's perfect justice demands that there is a price to be paid for that. Your friend finally gets that he can't afford it himself and he accepts the fact that he doesn't need to—that from beautiful grace, and through blood, God has already taken care of it all.

Your friend stands up. He turns and faces the half a dozen people blocking his path in the pew. They glance at him with what appear to be slightly judgmental eyes, but politely scoot in. He makes his way to the central aisle where he starts a very nerve-wracking walk towards the front.

It seems to me that long before he gets there, long before he prays with the pastor, that he's already acknowledged the need in his life and invited Christ into his heart! He's already a Christian. The actual prayer is just a ceremony of sorts.

EVEN WITH THE DECLARATION at the business conference, in my mind, my conversion was still unfinished business. The moment should be special and memorable. I was like a bride trying to create the dream wedding. Every detail mattered. And it was all starting to stress me out.

The location had to be just right. Should I go to the beach and look out on the vastness of the ocean or instead wait for a night when all the stars are shinning in the galaxy above?

What should I say? Should I write one down ahead of time or just wing it? Should I do it alone, or invite a friend? Richie, the former beer distributor, would be more than willing to come along, but I didn't want to infringe on his schedule. He has a family. Besides, the thought of having someone else there made me a little nervous. You know—what if I goofed things up?

Two weeks after coming home from the retreat, the details of what to do next were still plaguing me. One night, while driving my car down the main drag in Wilmington, my mind was once again going over all the possible scenarios: "Should I do this? Should I do that?" Suddenly my thoughts were interrupted by something foreign.

Christians always sound funny, bizarre, when they talk about something like this. I know such stories are hard to believe. If someone would have told me this when I was an Atheist I would have written him off as a nut. And yet this is what happened to me.

That foreign invasion was not exactly a voice. And it wasn't a thought either. It was more a sensation, a feeling that started in my stomach and just billowed up until it consumed my entire body. The feeling had words, but they weren't audible. All of a sudden, my train of thought had stopped and was replaced by something new that was taking me in an entirely different direction; "What are you worried about? It's done! It's taken care of! You got up in front of a group of strangers. You could have told them anything about yourself. You chose to tell them about me. You've done it! You're in! You belong to me now."

Confession: It Seemed Like Nothing Changed

Christianity is not for sissies. There's a toughness that outsiders may not understand. The walk is a constant hope and vision of the individual we're supposed to be and a painful reminder of the person we actually are. Over time, progress is made, the gap narrows, but at the end of the day there's always the realization of how much farther we have to go.

For me, life can feel like a tug-of-war between the old Doug and the new-and- improved version. Oh, how much I want to be a shining example of love, joy, peace, patience, kindness, goodness, faithfulness, gentleness and self-control. And oh, how much I miss the mark! Because more often than I care to admit, the Old Doug still comes out on top.

I AM NOT SURE exactly when this happened. It wasn't the day after realizing I was a Christian, but it couldn't have been too long after that.

I simply lost it at work. Just snapped! Totally went off on a young woman who works for me.

People yell in newsrooms all the time. It's the nature of the beast. The deadline pressure brings out the worst in us. Behavior that would be totally inappropriate in virtually any other field is considered normal in this business. It's not uncommon to see two people screaming at each other one hour and drinking with each other the next.

My victim was a young reporter right out of college. She was so afraid of making a mistake that she opted not to make any decisions at all. Everything she did was cleared first with management. As a member of management, that really got annoying. She called me seven, eight, nine times a day "What do you think about this? What should I do about that? Where am I supposed to go from here?"

On this particular day, she called at the worst possible time. She got me out of an important meeting. I didn't even listen to her latest question or give her a chance to talk. "I can't hold your hand forever! You're going to have to learn how to make a decision! You're going to have to figure this out!" *CLICK!*

The event shouldn't have fazed me, but it did. After all the spiritual Pomp and Circumstance, nothing had changed. I felt like a fraud. Here I was, this new Christian, acting like the same old guy. Where were all those fruits of the spirit? Where was the love, the peace, the patience, the kindness and self-control?

Maybe my conversion didn't "take." Maybe it wasn't real.

Hours later the conflict was still playing over and over again in my mind. I was so upset and worried that nothing had changed, that I failed to notice that something indeed was different. Being upset and worried was itself a change. I certainly had a long way to go, but being bothered and convicted by my actions was at least a step in the right direction.

Maybe God was working in me after all.

WHAT ABOUT YOU?

1. Take a sheet of paper (it doesn't have to be pink) and fold it into fours. Now describe the most important things in your life at age ten, ten years ago, today and ten years into the future

2. How have you publically shared your faith? What was the response and how similar was that to your expected response?

3. What is the one part of your life that you want God to fix most? How do you think he will do that?

10

GRADUALLY TO NEW

Every Sunday at my church, I moderate a discussion group called Starting Point. It is a ten-week course designed for individuals searching for God. Week after week, I hear people talk about the exact same issues and questions that used to bother me. I probably sound a lot like my mentor Richie: "Yep, I use to struggle with that too." Now, from my front-row seat, I get to watch as these individuals get beyond their sticking points. As they grow in their faith, my own faith grows.

And yet the people who inspire me the most, the ones who further my walk and bring me closer to God, are those dealing with something that goes far beyond my own experiences. Sometimes the hurdles that block their paths seem so much higher than what I faced. Often times I wonder if jumping over them is even an option.

"I almost didn't make it here today," a woman in her early twenties told the group one morning. "I was out with my friends last night. We were bar hopping. They started to make fun of me when I tried to leave early. They knew I wanted to go to church today. They coaxed me into staying till closing time."

It never occurred to me before, but listening to her story I realized that I was lucky and had a spiritual advantage that others don't. A big reason for me becoming a Christian was the fact that I moved to a new town. It's not that God's presence is more prevalent in Wilmington, North Carolina than in other places. It's just that no one knew me here. We moved as a family in March, went our separate ways in June and by late August I was a believer. That couldn't have happened in a town where people knew me—the old me.

First off all, there are those I've hurt. Because of the pain I've brought to their lives, news of me becoming a churchgoer would be greeted with skepticism. "Yeah, sure he is! That guy is incapable of changing. He is rotten to the core."

Even those who like me would have scoffed at the notion. They would hold the New Doug accountable for all the antics of the Old Doug. "Wait a minute. You're going to church? You're a Christian now? Oh, come on! Who do you think you're kidding? Aren't you the same guy who calls them 'Jesus Freaks' and 'Bible Thumpers?' And haven't I seen you naked? Remember streaking at the bar? Sure it was funny until you nearly got us all arrested. And now this naked, drunken, sarcastic guy is a Christian? Yeah, nice try!"

It seemed to me that the case of the young woman from the Starting Point class was a little bit different. Why didn't her friends want to let her go? The answer probably has less to do with that night and more to do with fears of the future. Watching someone move on means you're losing control over them, especially when they move on without you.

On some level, Jesus experienced this too. The Gospels tell the story of him failing. That's not a word you normally associate with Jesus, but it's there in the Bible. The book of

Luke says it happened towards the beginning of His ministry. Mathew and Mark have the same story somewhere closer to the middle. When it happened is not nearly as important as where it happened. The scene of Jesus' failure was His hometown of Nazareth, where the people knew Him best and perhaps loved Him the most.

As he's teaching in a synagogue, all the people become puzzled. The Bible says they're impressed by what He has to say and the fact that He has obtained all this knowledge. The Bible doesn't record the inner thoughts of those in the crowd, but reading the story you get a sense of what they're thinking: "Come on, who is He kidding? This is Joseph and Mary's boy. He's just a carpenter. Why should we listen to what He has to say?"

Getting nowhere, Jesus packs up and leaves. Before exiting Nazareth He turns to the disciples and says, "A prophet is honored everywhere except in His hometown and among His family and friends."

In order for the faith to grow, Jesus had to go.

Initially, I didn't give that young woman from the Starting Point class much of a chance. My heart went out to her, but her spiritual journey would be a tough one. She lacked the necessary support to keep her going. I was right about that, but wrong about the outcome.

She made a choice that must have been very hard. It's almost as if she took the advice of Mr. Tank. She figured out what the most important thing in her life was and then went about replacing the liabilities with assets. Her old friends were weeded out and new, more positive influences came into her life. For a long time she was very involved in our church, until she left to join the seminary.

As her faith grows, mine does too.

I often think of my own old friends. I've lost touch with so many of them over the years. If they think of me at all, it's memories of the Old Doug that come to mind. They are unaware of the transformation. It feels like part of me will always be stuck in the past.

That bothers me. As much as it was an advantage to be separated from them at the start of my walk, I'd like them to see that I've sincerely grown and changed. Besides, if they liked the Old Doug, I have a feeling they'd really like this new guy, too.

Part 6

The Law

"If one person falls, the other can reach out and help. But people who are alone when they fall are in real trouble."
(Ecclesiastes 4:10 NLT)

"For no one can be made right in God's sight by doing what His law commands. For the more we know God's law, the clearer it becomes that we aren't obeying it."
(Romans 3:20 NLT)

11

The Rules of the Game

A few moments after we finished presenting our pink sheets of paper, the entire business seminar broke for lunch. A guy, roughly around my age, who was sitting nowhere near me in the conference room, hunted me down and took the chair next to me in the dining area.

"Hey man, I just wanted to congratulate you. I don't know how many others got what you said. You know, who really understood what you meant by the word 'walk,' but I wanted you to know that I was one of them. Hearing your testimony made my day."

That's all he needed to say. I got his message. We spoke the same lingo. It was kind of like we were talking in code, or had a secret handshake, or wearing the same fraternity letters. In our own little way we were revealing that we were members of the same club.

Because of that commonality, we were free to open up and share other details of our lives. He told me about his family, his job, his church and even some funny stories about mission trips.

It was exciting. This was a new friend. I really liked this guy. We hit it off immediately. And it was all because I opened up and shared what was going on in my life.

Of course, just a few hours later, I absolutely hated the man.

HURDLE: THOU SHALL NOT

God is a prude.

I can't be the only one who's come to that conclusion. Just look at all the laws and rules he established. Sometimes it feels like he just handed them out in the hopes of tripping us up. In the secular world, laws are written to protect our rights and freedoms. Doesn't it sometimes seem like God's laws are there to limit our freedoms? It feels like he is saying, "Thou shall not have fun. Thou shall not enjoy life. Thou shall live a sterile and dull existence."

This is a big issue. It is almost a marketing problem. You probably know someone who's turned down your invitations to church, not because they doubt God's existence, but because the lifestyle of following him seems a little boring. To them, becoming a Christian means giving up some things that make life worth living.

Not me.

I was determined to do it my own way. Sure, I wanted to be a different person, to be nicer to people, to have a relationship with God, and to have him bless my life, but I wasn't going to let that interfere with my social calendar.

So, in the beginning, Christianity wasn't a way of life for me. It was more or less just an addition to my life.

SHE WAS A SURE THING.

Listen, I am no Casanova but I've been around long enough to know when a woman is attracted to me. This one was downright smitten. Okay, it could have been the vast amount of alcohol she consumed, but what does it matter? Either way, I was about to score.

At the end of the first day of the seminar, the Chamber held a social gathering. The point was to let us all mingle, to get to know each other outside of the conference room setting. They probably weren't expecting any of us to get sloppy drunk, but then again, it was an open bar.

An attractive woman introduced herself to me. Like the man I had met earlier in the day, she too was moved by my testimony. She had heard I went to the big non-denominational church in town and wanted to know what I thought of it. Did I like the music? Was it easy to make friends there? What did I think of the casual dress?

She told me that she attended a more traditional Baptist church across town. She had been going there for years and it did feel like home, but something had been telling her that it was time to move on.

This should have been a straightforward conversation. And it was—until the flirting started. I, inadvertently, said something funny and she laughed; that's when things got out of control. A big flaw of mine forms in the split second I realize there's an audience. It's like my entire personality changes. I instantly jump on stage. So, intentionally now, I said something funny and once again she laughed. This time, the humor resulted in her touching my shoulder, kind of brushing it in a tender, joking manner. The third time I made her chuckle, her hand slapped my knee.

Oh, yeah, this woman was a sure thing.

After a while the two of us got up to leave. There was a beach connected to the retreat, and we were planning on going for a moonlight walk. That was code talk too; I think we both knew what that really meant.

We didn't even make it to the door.

"Hey, where are you guys going?" It was my new Christian friend from lunch.

I didn't want to lie to him, but I certainly wasn’t going to tell him the truth. "I was just walking her back to her cabin.”

"Oh, don't worry about that. I'll take care of it."

And he did. He was the perfect gentlemen. He took her away and returned to the gathering a few minutes later. My night of passion was ruined. He knew exactly what he was doing. I could tell by the way he was looking at me when he came back. It wasn't exactly a smug or a smirk; it was more like his eyes were saying: "Hey, I am just trying to help out."

Who did he think he was? I wanted to go over and yell at him. "What are you doing? Who died and made you the Christian Cop of the world? We're grown adults here! Have you ever heard of the Man Code, buddy? You just violated the Man Code!"

Being a Christian didn't appear to be much fun.

HURDLE: DEVELOPING A DIFFERENT VISION

Where have all the prophets gone? Open up the Bible and you'll find story after story of men with the ability to look into the future. Actually, their gift was much more than that. The Biblical prophet was really a spokesperson for God. It seems to me, in these hectic times, we could really use more people speaking his will into our lives.

Oh, I know there are those who claim to be modern-day prophets. They write horoscope columns, run psychic hotlines, and host religiously based cable programs where they predict the end of the world for a small donation.

It's hard to get by all the fakes and phonies, but once you do, a truth emerges. There is such a thing as a modern-day prophet. They do exist. In fact I think they're all around us. They may not be what you expect. They actually come in the form of some very familiar faces. They're your friends who have the ability to see the path that you're on and the vision to look into the future and tell you where it leads. Oftentimes they add an entirely different perspective that goes far beyond your limited view. Because of that, they speak God's truth into your life, whether you like it or not, by offering warnings, advice and consultation.

Not much has changed. Having a prophet in your life is the same today as it was in Biblical times. In order to make use of their wisdom, you first have to be willing to listen to what they have to say.

THE NEXT MORNING, the object of my desire sat next to me at the business conference breakfast. We picked up where we left off. Once again I said something funny, and once again she laughed. As she did I instantly became thankful that nothing happened the night before. I don't know, maybe it was the hangover (that certainly had something to do with it), but I think even in a healthy state of mind I would have reached the same level of gratitude. You see, not to be rude, but the truth is this woman has the world's most annoying laugh.

She sounded like Woody Woodpecker going through Lamaze training; "Ha, ha, ha, HA, ha, eeew, eeew, EEEW!"

How in the world did I fail to notice it the night before? This wasn't a laugh. It wasn't even a cackle. It was just: "STOP! Please Stop!" For the first time in my life I had no desire to be funny. I started to talk about every serious subject I could think of: foreign policy, upcoming elections, Rheumatoid Arthritis. I even started to fake being all excited about the forthcoming seminar.

She wasn't buying any of it. "Ha ha ha HA ha, eeew, eeew, EEEW!"

What had I done to deserve this?

I didn't realize it at the time, probably didn't think about it until much later, but the night before and the morning after had something big in common. In both cases my vision was extremely limited. I was motivated only by the "now," living in the moment of "Get her in bed," or "Get me out of here." My thoughts did not extend very far into the future.

My Christian friend, the man I'd grown to hate, had much better eyesight. He wasn't just thinking about the next few hours, and he was preoccupied with more than just my own interest. That night he was able to look down the road and to see how it would all play out. After the romance was over he knew I would probably get a phone number and then never use it. He knew that the next time the group got together, in a month, it would be an awkward situation for this woman, for me and for everyone else. People would gossip about the "hook up." It would become a soap opera of sorts. The entire group may be split up into different sides, some choosing to root for her, others applauding my conquest. My friend saw the future and wanted to do something about it. As he watched from across the room, as the two us prepared to leave, he decided to act.

In this case, looking back, following God's rules was best for everyone.

I should probably thank that Christian friend of mine, whom I no longer hate. And I'd do it too, but the Man Code forbids me from being sappy and emotional.

Confession: I Break More Rules as a Believer than I ever did as a Nonbeliever

As an Atheist I never sinned. Never! At least, not as far as I was concerned. You see, not believing in God came with the fringe benefit of also not believing in sin. If it didn't exist in my mind, how could I commit it with my body? Oh, there were laws, police and a judicial system, but provided I stayed out of jail, nothing I did could possibly be all that bad.

That luxury started fading away when I became a Christian. It wasn't all at once; it happened little by little over time. God is always revealing some new blemish He wants me to focus on. It works like this: the better I get to know Him and understand His glory, the more I am aware of my own flaws and shortcomings.

That could come across as self-defeating, like you are being set up to fail. But through it all is this undeniable sense of love. It is an overpowering love that doesn't focus on how far you need to go. Instead it allows you to look back and see how far you've already been carried.

IT LOOKED LIKE a definite scam. The name on the friend request was totally unfamiliar. We had no mutual acquaintances. This had to be the work of some con artist trying to gain access to my personal information. The smart thing was to quickly hit the delete button, but there was something about the profile picture that was inviting.

The hair was much shorter, the eyes were now accompanied by laugh lines, and even though the face had aged it was still very beautiful. It took a few moments, the brain had to process the fact that married women change their last names, but eventually I put it all together: Chisel had found me online.

It seemed totally unreal. We had only known each other a few months. Twenty years had passed since our last encounter. I didn't even think that she would remember me, much less reach out in my direction. But there she was, as if sent by God, to help answer the unresolved questions.

Her life didn't go as planned, but then does anybody's? She kept the baby, a little girl, but other than writing a monthly check, the father was totally out of the picture. She remained close to her parents. They were there during the hard years offering support, love, and the occasional helping hand as Amy put herself through school. In time she would meet another man, fall in love, get married and have two more children.

The catching up was fun, but eventually I had to ask the question that had been plaguing me. I had to know if she was still a woman of faith. "Oh, I'm still a believer. Always have been," she told me one night on the phone. "Don't get me wrong. There were times I wondered if my life was just too small and insignificant for God to pay attention to it." She then added as an afterthought with no knowledge of how much it would hit home to me: "But somehow I always knew that He was never too far away. I didn't exactly follow all the rules, or do things the right way, but through it all, when I needed it the most, His love was always there giving me the strength to go on."

WHAT ABOUT YOU?

1. How do you view God's rules and laws?

2. What friends will hold you accountable? In what ways do you hold each other accountable?

3. What sin have you won victory over, and how can you be sure? In what areas of your life is God currently asking you to submit to Him?

12

Gradually to Follower

This may be a controversial statement, but I think it's easier for people with children to understand God's love. Parents have learned that the word "no" can be said with affection. They also have to impose rules and enforce the consequences when they're broken.

From a very early age, my son loved to swim. One day, when he was two years old, we were walking to the pool at my apartment complex. In his excitement he got ahead of me. He was running out into the parking lot, trying to make it to our destination as quickly as possible.

"Whoa! Whoa! Whoa! Whooooa!" I frantically was trying to catch up. It took only a few seconds for me to cover the ground between us, but it was long enough for a horrible scenario to play out in my mind. I could hear the screeching of the breaks. In truth, no car was approaching but the dreadful sound was ringing in my ears anyway. I physically felt the impact and saw the blood on the pavement. The sirens of a rushing ambulance were already blaring in the background, and I could even smell that sterile hospital scent.

The panic attack didn't seem like a spiritual event, but it actually exposed a huge truth about God. Where once I saw the rules as limitations or sacrifices, they now appeared to be an incredible sign of his love. The same type of love that prompted the first commandment of my son's life, "Thou shall look both ways before crossing the street. I am your Father, the Dad Almighty!"

In that moment I moved from someone with no intention of obeying God's rules, at least the ones I didn't like, to an individual who was completely overwhelmed by how much He actually cared for me. I stopped seeing the laws as God's excuse to bring down His wrath when I did something wrong. At the same time, they could no longer be used as a bargaining chip for my advantage when I did something right: "Come on, God, I've been so good. You have to honor my prayer."

Our relationship had transformed into that of a father and child. His concerns were the same of all parents. He didn't want to see me get hurt, and couldn't bear the thought of me getting run over by bad decisions. If I listened to His words, maybe I could finally stay out of trouble.

All of this was lost on my son. He instantly started to cry the moment I stopped him. He just looked up at me with these sad, blue eyes that appeared to say, "What's the big deal? Why are you so mad?" To him, if only for a brief moment, he must have felt like our relationship was severed by rules and consequences. Did he even wonder if his father still loved him?

There is a great story on this topic, it's split into two areas of the Bible. I have a polar-opposite reaction to each part. After the first half I'm angry at God. I want to yell, "What's your deal? Take a chill pill! Get over yourself!" Then, when I get to the conclusion, told in an entirely separate book of the Bible, I am once again reminded of his tenderness. Both extremes can be found in the life of Moses.

Here is a guy who does everything asked of him. He gets his people out of Egypt, parts the Red Sea, distributes the Ten Commandments and wanders the desert for forty years all the while tolerating a nagging, bickering, complaining flock. His leadership and direction are always questioned and scrutinized. One day, as told in the book of Numbers, Moses gets fed up. He's had enough! In his anger, while performing a miracle on God's behalf, he bangs a stick into a rock. "Sorry, buddy," God tells Moses, "You can't get into the Promised Land now."

That hardly seems fair. Where's the compassion? Why wasn't God more understanding? How could he let one, small infraction ruin the relationship with this man who had done so much for Him?

The conclusion of the story is in the next book, Deuteronomy.

God takes Moses up to a mountain to give him a glimpse of the land he's forbidden to enter. That may sound cruel, almost like he's teasing Moses, but there's love in God's action. From that vantage point Moses could look out and see the Jordan Valley, the City of Jericho and beyond that the Mediterranean Sea.

Imagine what God must have been whispering in Moses' ear, "Look, isn't it beautiful? This was what the entire struggle was about. You weren't just wandering; I was leading you here. There's plenty of food down there. Your people are going to prosper. Eventually, they're going to turn their back on me, but I know you never did. You made it to the finish line! I can't let you cross because you broke a rule, and there are consequences for that, but I wanted you to see what you accomplished." And then perhaps he added the words that so many grown adults long to hear from their father, "I am proud of you, son."

The Bible says Moses died on that mountain top. But you have to believe that he left this world knowing that the love of his Father was still very much intact.

As for me, that night at the business conference would not be the last time I would break God's rules. But the struggle was about to get a lot easier. Help was on the way.

Part 7

Transformation

"Let God transform you into a new
person by changing the way you think.
Then you will know what God wants
you to do, and you will know how
good and pleasing and perfect His will
really is."
(Romans 12:2 NLT)

"Those who become Christians become
new persons. They are not the same anymore,
for the old life is gone. A new life has begun."
(2 Corinthians 5:17)

13

When God Became Real

I know the God I rejected. There's a clear and vivid picture of Him in my mind. I actually know Him better than the one I later accepted. The one that was cast aside was the "Old Man in the Sky." His job was to keep me in line when my parents weren't watching. He was eventually written off because His love was fickle and he seemed all too eager to throw down a lighting bolt when I got out of control.

The God I accepted is vastly different, and He's still a mystery to me. I'm unable to wrap my arms (and brain for that matter) around who He is and what role He's supposed to play in my life. The metaphors used to describe Him don't help at all in this regard. They only add to my confusion. Is he a King, Lord, Creator, Supreme Being?

All of this is a real problem. If I can't define and understand who or what I believe in, then how can I really believe in Him? Will doubt always be a part of my life? If only there was a way to make God tangible and real. But how does one go about that?

Sometimes, I go to the beach and stare at the vastness of the ocean just hoping that God's presence will engulf me. When it doesn't work, I'll look down and pick up a seashell and study its intricacies. I am always in awe that the same being could be responsible for something so massive and powerful as well as something so fine and detailed. But neither creation makes me feel closer to God.

There's a neighborhood park that has special meaning to me. That's where, right after the breakup, a stranger at the swimming pool first invited me to his church. On paper, this sentimental place would appear to be an obvious place for me to bond with God. Often times I go there to think over my problems. I always leave feeling better, but the truth is, God has never spoken to me at this site.

The Bible, at times, gives me hope. There've been so many occasions when it felt like I was reading the exact line of scripture at the precise right moment in time. Was this of God's doing, all part of His plan? Why then, wasn't He more consistent? What about those times when I really needed His guidance only to turn to the Bible and read a long, tedious section, telling me how to sacrifice a lamb or a goat?

Eventually I did find God. The search probably lasted longer than it should have, because He was hanging out in the most unusual of locations. I found Him inside of me.

HURDLE: MAY THE FORCE BE WITH YOU

All my life I've heard people talk about "The Father, Son and the Holy Spirit." Two out of three were easy to understand, but the third one never really made sense.

Maybe my confusion was a side effect of being born in the 1970s. I think Star Wars *tainted my vision of God. I was a child when the film was released, and haven't seen it since, but one particular line from that movie has stuck with me: "May the force be with you." That seemed to imply that the force was some cosmic wave in the atmosphere. For it to be "with you" it had to float in your direction. Did the Holy Spirit work in the same fashion?*

Under this notion, like a real estate agent trying to sell a house, location is everything. If you're in the right place, sometimes the spirit finds you. It pleasantly smacks you in the face leading to days of great luck and good fortune. At other moments it skips over you completely, choosing instead to land on someone else. Doesn't this explain the randomness of life? Maybe it even explains why a tornado will destroy one house and leave the one next-door untouched.

The first time someone told me that the Spirit was actually living inside of me, I was totally spooked out. "What do you mean? Someone other than me is in my body?" This version seemed far more sci-fi than the one created by George Lucas. And yet the explanation instantly answered another riddle in my mind. If true, this would make sense of how God could keep track of every event, thought and detail in my life and everyone else's. Maybe He wasn't watching a bunch of little ants from way up above; maybe he (or at least a part of Him) was going through life with us, inside of us.

MY EX WAS IN A BAD PLACE. Five months had come and gone since the breakup and her life really hadn't moved on. It was now clear that she was regretting her decision. Maybe she missed me. Perhaps she was looking at our past and focusing more on the pleasant memories. When the ugly ones, now long removed, came into her mind they were probably downplayed. She may have concluded, "He really wasn't such a bad guy after all."

She was also having money issues. Her current financial situation probably went a long way in blocking out the pain of the past. As much as my heart and ego wanted to be fooled into thinking that she was yearning for me, my head knew that wasn't the case. She was really longing for that sense of stability that comes when the bills get paid.

Her motives didn't matter to me because mine, too, were less than pure. This was the opportunity to get back the one thing I wanted most in the world. This was my chance to be reunited with my son on a full-time basis, to watch him grow up and to stop worrying about what would happen to our joint custody arrangement when he got old enough to attend school. You strike when the iron is hot, or in this case, when the woman is vulnerable. And so, I picked up the phone and asked her out.

In any event, I needed a date. There was this formal charity ball that work was making me attend. It was the type of function where you dare not show up alone. Plus this was exactly the sort of thing she would like. She could feel glamorous for a night, get all dressed up, enjoy a nice dinner and an evening of dancing. There was virtually no hesitation before she accepted my offer.

A few days later, on my lunch break, I was going to get measured for a tuxedo. That's when the plan started to unfold. My body was taken over by a foreign invader. It wasn't an entirely new sensation. The same thing had happened, in the car once before, when I was struggling to figure out the perfect way to accept Christ. But this time, whatever was speaking to me, took on a totally different tone. On that first night, He sounded like a pleasant and reassuring motivational speaker who wanted me to relax and quit worrying so much. On this occasion He was downright rude and confrontational. His message came in the form of a simple question: "How is this going to play out?"

"What do you mean, play out?" Even though the voice I heard wasn't exactly audible, that didn't stop me from answering the question out loud. I must have looked crazy. Who knows what the driver in the car next to me thought? "It's simple. We go to the ball. We have a good time."

It was like this pestering, nagging thing inside knew he was dealing with a journalist. Maybe he was one too. He certainly mastered the art of the follow-up question: "And then what?"

HURDLE: TAPPING IN

Does everyone get the same amount of the Holy Spirit? It certainly feels like some of my friends were blessed with more than me. Did God hand pick a few people and fill up their spiritual tanks while the rest of us got some lesser amount? I am not being facetious here. This is something I really think about.

The example of my pastor would support the argument that some get more than others. He's the real thing. He accepted Christ at a young age, and has spent his life trying to follow where the Spirit leads him. Perhaps it's no surprise that like many professional Christians, he inherited the family business. His father was also in the ministry, which leads me to wonder if being engulfed by the Spirit is just a genetic trait passed down from one generation to the next like eye or hair color.

On the other side of the spectrum is my mentor Richie, the former beer distributor. He's only been walking a few years longer than me. And yet, he moves through the Spirit as if he's been doing it his entire life. How did he get so far so fast? Sometimes I think he must be like a body builder doing his daily reps, building this thing inside of him by reading the Bible and connecting with God in prayer.

Even though these two guys came from different backgrounds, even though one met God virtually at birth and the other not until he was an adult, they both managed to arrive at the same blessed destination: a Spirit-filled life.

Maybe the pastor was given more than me. Maybe the beer distributor excelled faster through endurance and heavy lifting. But the biggest thing that separates us has nothing to do with quantity. Instead, it's that these two guys have learned something I haven't quite mastered yet. They know the quantity doesn't matter, if you haven't first figured out how to tap into it.

IT WAS EASY to answer the follow-up question. I was way ahead of God on this one. The next step was a big part of my plan. It was why things were put in motion in the first place. "After the dance we'll get back together and eventually she'll move in with me." My ex was now living in a rural area a hundred miles away, making our joint custody very complicated.

"And then what?" The nagging wasn't going away.

"Oh, I see where you're going. Is that what you're worried about?" I was almost embarrassed by the oversight. My plan did not cover this topic, but I could deal with it:

"I'm a changed person. This time I'll do it the right way. Sure, if that's what you want, I'll marry her."

"And then what?"

No matter what I said, or how I answered it, this foreign invader kept coming back with the same three words. It was really getting annoying: "And then what? And then what? And then what?" My plan to reunite with my son did not include all this scrutiny. The tuxedo shop was only a mile away, but things were crumbling all around me. Like it or not, this exercise was showing me that the path I was about to go down would lead to more problems and pain.

Here is how it would all unfold: "And then she would get pregnant. And then she would refuse to quit partying. And then we would fight over her friends. And then we would fight over the money. And then I would start worrying about other men. And then we would break up, again. And then two children, not one, would grow up in a broken home. And then I would be in the exact same position that I am today, older but not wiser."

The words "conclusion" and "outcome" have the same basic meaning but sometimes they can be different. In this case the drawn-out conclusion was not a pretty picture. And yet, the outcome was one of the most beautiful moments in my life.

As the world's foremost expert on my own thoughts and feelings, I knew whatever was going on inside me was not *of* me. My brain just doesn't work like that. It doesn't see that far ahead. Once it had taken the foresight of a stranger at a business conference to keep me from making a mistake; now I was able to see the future by myself. Sort of. You see, even though I was alone, I knew that I was anything but on my own.

And so my beautiful outcome was that the search was finally over. God's whereabouts were no longer a mystery. I had found Him. He was real and tangible. He wasn't hanging out at the beach or at some sentimental neighborhood park. He wasn't floating around the atmosphere either. In all His wisdom, He decided to be more accessible than that. He had become a part of me.

CONFESSION: IT'S NOT ENOUGH TO JUST GET ADVICE FROM THE SPIRIT

Eventually the Spirit changes how He communicates with you. At least He did for me. It transformed in both volume and message.

The first several times I felt this sensation invading my body, whether it was the reassuring motivational speaker or the confrontational friend, it always felt like someone was hitting me over the head with a sledge hammer: Boom! "Ouch! What was that?"

Slowly, as the gap between the person I am and the one I'm supposed to be started to narrow, the feeling became subtle and gentler. Sometimes now, it's barely louder than a faint whisper. These days I am often left to wonder if the tingling is really God trying to prompt me in a certain direction or if it could possibly be something I had for lunch.

The other change is far more significant. The messages were once all about me. The Spirit offered up great advice on what to do, or more often what not to do. It was then my responsibility to follow through. But that wasn't good enough. Eventually God started to pepper in a different line of thinking. There's no way to prevent it; in time God's spirit will get you to think of others and how you can help them.

Sure, I long for those shouted and undeniable sledge hammer sensations. But more than that, I am impatient for what's still to come: that day when other people are the focus of all my thoughts and actions. If I make it to that point, I will arrive at a time when Jesus isn't just living inside of me, He is actually living through me.

DON'T GET THE WRONG IDEA. It's not like I pulled the car over and immediately called my ex to cancel our plans.

However, the truth is: I never did make it to the tuxedo shop that day.

Still, it was almost a week before the phone call was placed. Perhaps I was giving God time to change his mind and endorse my plan. Eventually, that hope was discarded.

She didn't take it well. She was mad at me and maybe even a little bit hurt. One day, God willing, she will realize that in all the years we've known each other, not taking her to the ball was the biggest act of love I ever offered her.

WHAT ABOUT YOU?

1. Describe the first time you felt the Spirit moving in you? What about the most recent time?

2. What is your typical response when you sense a prompting?

3. Describe a time when you felt the Spirit moving you with thoughts and concerns for someone else.

14

Gradually to Surrender

You know what's strange? It is so much easier for me to surrender to God's will when I am worried about a major event, one that pushes me to the limit and causes me to take drastic change. It is in the smaller, seemingly insignificant moments, when nothing is hanging in the balance, that I am more likely to go my own way.

The first time my pastor invited me to lunch I was a nervous wreck. Just the thought of carrying out a long conversation with a "man of God" was terrifying. What if I said something stupid? What if I accidently dropped a swear word? What if he gave me a pop quiz on the Bible?

When you're under intense pressure to perform, you look for a safety net wherever you can find one. Mine came from an old business card hidden beneath my driver's seat. I was cleaning out the car trying to get it ready for my passenger. The name and number on the front of the card weren't at all familiar, but I instantly recognized its value as a social gold mine. You see, next to the contact information was a picture of a guy on a surfboard.

You've got to understand. My pastor is a huge surfer. He talks about his hobby all the time, even working it into his sermons on Sunday morning.

If I could somehow get him to comment about the card, the two of us could have a wonderful conversation. So, my fingers strategically placed this security blanket, front end up, in a section of the console. It would be impossible for anyone to miss it.

It was only there for a split second when that sledge hammer started pounding me on the back of the head. "You don't need to do that. The two of you have *me* in common. That's more than enough."

I didn't bother to argue my side. Instead, I started shaking my head violently hoping the thought would disappear. Anyway, why was God even wasting His time with something so trivial? His counsel was appreciated when it prevented me from making a major mistake, but I could handle something like driving to lunch on my own. The card stayed exactly where I left it.

Does a business card have anything in common with an apple?

The story of Adam and Eve has always bothered me. Really, all our modern-day problems are the results of two people eating an apple? Put that notion on the scales of justice and tell me how it all adds up. Doesn't the punishment far outweigh the crime? *CRUNCH!* Now there are earthquakes, famine and disease? *CRUNCH!* Now there's jealousy, hatred and murder?

To me, God comes across looking much worse in this story than the first man and woman he places on Earth. If He didn't want them to eat the fruit, then why did He put the tree there in the first place? Was He just setting them up to fail? If the Bible teaches us to forgive, why does God get away with holding such a petty grudge?

For the longest time Adam and Eve, with many other stories of the Old Testament, were pushed to some dark corner of my mind. I focused instead on the Gospels and the letters written by Paul. But little-by-little, an appreciation for the older stories started to form. They were no longer written off as fables or metaphors. They now took on a totally different meaning. I even started to accept them as historical facts. When it came to the events in the Garden of Eden, I ended up switching sides.

So often we judge sin and give it weight based on the crime. A white lie is easy to acquit. A brutal murder is much harder to forgive. To God it's all the same. He is far less concerned about the act of sin. He instead focuses on its cause, which is almost always the same. To Him it is never an issue of degree; it is always a matter of trust.

You see, if I am honest then Adam and Eve aren't the only ones at fault for the condition of the world. Some of the blame belongs on me. By leaving a business card face up in a console, I, too, took a bite of the apple. *CRUNCH!*

Yes, I've wondered why, if I wasn't supposed to use it for my advantage, that He allowed me to find the card in the first place. We could have avoided the conflict if only it had stayed hidden. Who knows? Maybe he was testing me, or exposing my lack of trust by revealing on the smallest levels.

It's funny, my pastor never saw the photograph of the surfer, or if he did, it never came up in conversation. Looking back, that's a good thing: "Hey, do you surf?"

"Nope! Never have. Frankly, I prefer activities that actually require athletic skill, like golf or softball." That's not exactly the perfect ice breaker!

It doesn't matter if it's a whisper or that sledge hammer sensation, or if it's something big or rather small. Every time the Spirit moves us, our lives are placed on a crossroads. The old me, version 1.0, collides head on with the new creation. We can either take a few more steps in our walk, or move backwards by biting the apple.

Sometimes, as I was about to discover, the collision at the intersection is anything but a metaphor.

PART 8

GRACE

"If you are good, is this some great gift
to Him? What could you possibly give Him?
(Job 35:7 NLT)

"God saved you by his special favor when
you believed. And you can't take credit
for this; it is a gift from God. Salvation is not
a reward for the good things we have done so
none of us can boast about it."
(Ephesians 2:8-9 NLT)

15

Shipyard and Burnett

You should see my Bible. It's in horrible condition, all banged up and falling apart. The front and back covers disappeared long ago. The pages are still in place, but probably not for long. The glue on the binding is fading away, and eventually duct tape will be required to keep everything together.

The time has come to get a new one, but it would be hard to part with this particular Bible. It has a lot of special meaning to me. Yes, it is a sentimental object, but far beyond that, it serves as a record of my innermost spiritual thoughts and my connection with God. Passages are underlined, highlighted, circled and bracketed in a variety of different colored ink.

Some Christian friends of mine get offended by the appearance of my Bible. These are the type of people who buy a hand-bound, calfskin edition and then place inside another leather case. In their eyes, a shabby-looking Bible means I have no respect for the words it contains. Plus, they're always wondering why my Bible is covered in blood.

Oh, if only I had better business sense! There's a scam to be had here, one that would make a ton of money. All I'd have to do is to proclaim that the blood magically appeared one day. "It must be a sign from God! He wants to remind us that we are covered in the blood of his Son!" You know people would flock to my house in droves. They'd come from all over. They'd arrive on my front porch with their crutches and goiters just wanting to see and touch the miracle. And I'd let them, for a small fee.

It's tempting, not just for all the easy money but for another very good reason. Even if the scam turned me into a false prophet, at least I wouldn't have to admit the truth. The real version of the story, of how the blood actually got on the Bible, makes me look incredibly stupid. It's there because I failed to look to the left.

HURDLE: EVERYONE NEEDS A SAVIOR

The hardest part about sharing the Gospels in this country is that most Americans feel they already know the story. Every December they learn about Jesus' birth. Every spring they're reminded of his death and resurrection. They know he was born of a virgin, that he walked on water and performed a variety of other miracles, and that he died on the cross for their sins. Witnessing is doomed to fail if it's only a recap of something outsiders have heard a thousand times before.

"Yeah, but they don't get it!" some argue, "Because if they did, clearly they would feel the same way that I do." And so these believers start in on the same song and dance with the confidence that this time, because it is coming from them, the explanation will really make sense.

That's fine—I guess. I applaud their efforts and determination. But to be successful, Christians first have to understand that the disconnect comes not from a lack of knowledge on the part of the listener. Therefore the telling of the Gospels must be more than a recitation of the facts.

The trick is to not to explain what happened, instead it is to expose the beauty hidden beneath what so many have already heard.

THE ACCIDENT has replayed itself over and over again in my mind, and even after all this time I am not exactly sure what went wrong. I just have to chalk it up to a momentary lack of judgment.

My car was on Burnett Street heading south in the industrial part of Wilmington. About a half mile down the road, at Shipyard Boulevard, was a semi truck waiting to turn. It had been sitting there for a while with no sign of oncoming traffic. The driver had to be waiting on me. Trucks of that size need enough room to make wide turns and he couldn't do that until I got out of his way and freed up the lane. And so at the stop sign I paused for a second and then proceeded to move forward.

I remember the noise. It's still vivid in my mind: the honking of the horn and the screeching of the brakes. That's when I glanced up to the left and saw the front grill of another semi truck barreling directly towards me. "This is not good!" You won't believe that, but honestly those were the exact words that came out of my mouth. (Afterwards I actually bragged to church friends that when death was staring me in the face, I made it through the fear without cussing. On a day that will be remembered for my stupidity, at least I can be proud of that one fact.)

What happened next is a little vague. I have no recollection of the actual impact, of metal hitting metal, of my side of the car caving in, of the shattering of glass, of being thrown to the passenger side or my bloody head landing on the open Bible. It all happened within a fraction of a second.

People don't walk away from a wreck like this one. You see a big eighteen-wheeler embedded into a little Chevy and the natural assumption is that someone was killed or at least seriously injured. However, there I was standing on my own two feet, looking over the damage and waiting for an ambulance that really wasn't needed.

It's standard procedure. At least that's what the medics said as they strapped me to a gurney and rushed me away with sirens blaring. Convinced that there must be internal bleeding, or perhaps a severe concussion, the doctors gave me two sets of X-rays but found nothing. After stitching up my head, they admitted me for what they called "an observational period."

Richie, the onetime beer distributor and current spiritual mentor, came by for a visit. We joked how this clearly wasn't "my time" and how it must be a sign that God had a plan for me. And then he took my hand and prayed, "Heavenly Father, we just want to thank you for being with Doug and looking out for him."

He wasn't through, but that's all he really needed to say. With those words my entire perspective changed. Even though months earlier I had accepted the Cross and what Jesus did for me, I now understood the beauty of how it really pertained to my life.

Oh, it had nothing to do with the obvious parallels. It wasn't like my mind drew the lines and connected the dots between my life being saved in this world and the realization of needing a savior in the next. It's unclear to me if the real beauty is simpler than that, or far more complex. It has nothing to do with salvation and everything to do with being unworthy.

As Richie was continuing on in prayer, my mind had stopped listening to him and instead was embracing how undeserving I was to be alive, to be in that room, to have the fellowship of a friend and the promise of tomorrow. Those notions were no longer considered rights, or anything I was entitled to; they had become incredible gifts that far exceeded my own value. Nothing I did that day earned me a second chance: I didn't wear my seatbelt, wasn't paying attention, failed to look both ways. I was alive not because of my actions, but in spite of them.

Honestly, it was the most beautiful realization in the world. One where the only proper response is unadulterated gratitude. But prior to that moment, I had failed to view the Cross in the same way.

Truth is, I thought I could buy my salvation. It was just a matter of volunteering enough hours at church, reading the Bible on a daily basis, joining a small group, being diligent in prayer, journaling, listening to the Spirit, doing my best to follow the rules and generally being an all around nice guy. Eventually, if I kept going and going and going, there'd be a finish line where Jesus didn't need to pay for my sins. Instead, that tab would be charged to the account of my great deeds and efforts.

If it was true that nothing I did that day earned me my life, then something else was now also very obvious. Nothing I could possibly do in the future would ever make me deserving of what happened on the Cross.

My relationship with Jesus was once again at a crossroads. I could no longer try, so desperately hard, to be worthy of all His love. From here on out, it was just up to me to receive it.

Hurdle: The New Beginning

Not too long ago, I got into a debate with a friend over the importance of the resurrection. We're both Christians who believe that Jesus rose from the grave. We just disagree on why that was such an important event.

My friend is a bright guy. As an intellectual, he appreciates the events recorded in the Bible for their historic impact. For him, the resurrection matters because it was the ultimate marketing tool. By conquering the grave, Jesus proved that He was who He claimed to be. My friend argues that without this victory, Christianity never would have gotten off the ground. The book of Acts appears to agree with Him. It has several passages where the earliest believers seem shaken by the crucifixion. "Had He not come back to them," my friend points out, "they wouldn't have had the courage and strength to start a church or much less a movement that ultimately changed the world."

He's right. Of course he is. But I've always felt that the resurrection has a meaning that goes far beyond Biblical times. It has to matter today, in this world and to my 21st century life.

To me, it's all about a promise from God. It's like a money-back guarantee that a relationship with him will change your life, that you will never be the same again. On the cross Jesus wiped our slate clean of not just sin, but if we're willing to let go, also our past. Three days later, when He rose again, He gave us the type of hope that only comes with a new beginning.

Yes, the resurrection has great historic value, but as far as I am concerned it will always be far more about the future than it is about the past.

RICHIE WASN'T THE ONLY VISITOR at the hospital. The cop working the accident also showed up. He was an intimidating character, but when you're in the wrong, every police officer fits into that category.

"How long have you lived in North Carolina?" There was no light shining in my face, but his tone made it clear that this was an interrogation. “You’ve been here eight or nine months, right? So why do you still have a Louisiana license? And your insurance expired four months ago. You know I could throw you in jail for all this.”

There was a long pause. He may have been waiting for me to say something, but I dared not speak. Besides, the only response going through my mind sounded totally sarcastic: “Well, I know that now!”

He took out his ticket book, sat down in a chair next to the bed, and allowed his face to soften. “Okay, I am not going to write up anything on the insurance. Your car’s totaled, and that’s enough punishment for not having coverage. I am going to overlook the seatbelt thing too; honestly that probably saved your life. Otherwise you would have been trapped on the driver’s side and been crushed to death. I should give you something for not registering in the state.” He considered it for a moment and then concluded, “Just promise me you’ll get a North Carolina license in thirty days and we’ll call it even. Consider yourself very lucky.” He ripped just one page out of the book and handed it to me. “All you’re getting is this—‘Failure to Yield.’”

Several weeks later, the mercy shown by the officer was duplicated by the Assistant District Attorney in court. He threw out the only remaining citation because he predicted that the trucking company would sue. He told me you can’t have an accident these days without someone filing a suit.

There should have been tons of gratitude on my part, but there wasn’t. Instead I was filled with fear. The threat that a man carrying a subpoena could one day show up at work haunted me. It was the type of thing that is always on your mind, even when you’re not thinking about it; it’s still there lurking beneath the surface.

My friends kept telling me to "surrender it," but they didn't understand. It was only a matter of time before things were going to get worse.

The stress was taking over. For a while I couldn't sleep, couldn't eat. At work I started to research bankruptcy protection and gave up all hope that I'd ever get out of debt, own a home, or become financially stable.

The fear consumed me to such a degree that the reality of the situation was completely lost. It didn't matter that day after day, week after week, even month after month slipped by with no sign of an unwanted visitor armed with legal documents. You cannot have hope for the future when you allow yourself to be lost in the past.

And so a year was wasted.

The statute of limitations for civil action expired on the anniversary of the wreck. At that moment I could feel the weight being lifted off my shoulders. The consequences of all that went wrong, the combination of lack of judgment and stupid mistakes, were finally let go. Looking back, it's pretty clear that I had been the only one who was holding on to them. Even though the police officer, the Assistant District Attorney, the truck driver and the company that employed him had forgiven me, it took a year for me to believe their pardon was for real. Not accepting had a stifling effect.

It's strange: in Christianity it's easy to get stuck too. Some of us focus so much on what Jesus did on the Cross that we fail to arrive at the rest of the story. While his sacrifice is hugely important, if you never get to the resurrection and live it out in your walk, it is almost as if Jesus died in vain. And so you must move on. Every believer needs to experience a second acceptance where they fully embrace his promise of a new life.

In my case, when I finally reached that point, I found that my Savior had been patiently waiting for me all along. He was now ready to show me how to follow his lead by teaching me to rise again.

Confession: Sometimes the Beauty Fades

Ask any married couple that's been together for a long time and they'll all tell you the same thing. "It's tough. It's a lot of hard work." In reality they are describing every relationship and all types of love.

The world moves at such a quick pace that it threatens to gloss over the beauty of something that once captivated you. A once great and powerful love can easily be lost in the everyday shuffle of life. Problems at the office, at home, with your health and even goals or ambitions for the future have the capacity to alter your focus and to take you away from the thing you treasure the most.

Faith, like marriage, takes a lot of dedication. Your only hope is to keep the romance alive.

I STILL DO ALL THE THINGS I did before and more. Still volunteer at church, read the Bible, enjoy the fellowship of Christian friends, pray, journal, listen to worship music and wake up early to spend quiet time with God. Of course my motives have changed. It is no longer a fruitless attempt at being worthy. They are now genuine efforts to be closer to my Heavenly Father. But just like before, it is never enough.

All it takes is just a little distraction. Sometimes it comes in the form of stress; at other moments it can be a project that grabs my attention. Either way, all of a sudden, my devotions get sidelined. If I stay on this path too long it becomes clear that something is missing. Life, once again, is robbed of all forward momentum and feels very stagnant.

The good news is when the distance seems too much to handle, there's one remedy that never fails. All I have to do is take the long way into work. There's always a collision with God waiting for me at the corner of Shipyard and Burnett. I pray that never changes. At the crossroads, I am once again reminded of the beauty of being unworthy and his promise of a new beginning.

WHAT ABOUT YOU?

1. How have you tried to be worthy of the Cross? How do you get to the point where you can let go of these fruitless efforts?

2. In what ways are you holding on to the past? How has this kept you from rising again?

3. What do you have in your life: a location, an item, or a memory that can serve as a reminder to what God has already done for you? Explain why its importance.

16

GRADUALLY TO ACTION

The crash was not the typical near-death experience. There was never an out-of-body ordeal where my soul was floating towards the proverbial white light. All the same, being hit by a semi-truck is as close to death as I wish to get for the next several decades.

Surviving something that should have killed you can come with the side effect of unwanted stress and pressure. You start wondering why you were spared. Did God leave you down here because there's unfinished business? Does he have a special plan for you? Does he want you to accomplish or do something great on his behalf?

It's strange I didn't lose my life in the wreck, but it no longer really belonged to me. My life was now God's possession. To do with whatever He saw fit.

He could have asked for anything. If He wanted me to pack up and become a missionary, that could be arranged. If He nudged me into quitting my job to join the seminary, I was willing. If He had whispered in my ear to feed the homeless, a food drive would have been organized the next day. But none of that happened. Instead of detailed instructions, God, for some unknown reason, chose to remain silent.

Why?

This seemed a little out of character for Him. Story after story in the Bible depicts God as someone who pays very close attention to the details. He wasn't shy about giving specific orders to Noah, Moses and Joshua. He told them to build this, say that, or go there.

In the book of Joshua, God takes micro-managing to an extreme. At long last the Israelites were going to enter the Promised Land. The only thing standing in their way was a muddy, overflowing Jordan River. God was very specific on how his people were to cross. He wanted the Arc to go first. Twelve priests, six on each side, were told to carry the Covenant. The others were required to follow several hundred yards behind.

To be sure, even with all the instructions, success required an undeniable belief in God. After all, two individuals had to be the first ones to place their feet into the flooding waters moving at a rapidly dangerous current. You can see these two guys, can't you? Each one standing directly across from the other, I'll bet you their eyes met in a moment of fear. They probably shared a glance, a hesitant expression, a deep breath and then slowly blowing it out through lips that trembled on the exhale. They didn't have to say a word to each other. Their faces probably revealed what they were both thinking: "Are we really going to do this?" And then, somehow, they pushed their anxiety aside and together took a leap of faith.

Lifting up their feet, and then placing them back down in the water, took a tremendous amount of courage, but was it really that big of a deal? All they did is what God specifically told them to do.

The faith they displayed was similar to dancing the Hokey Pokey. If only God was always so crystal clear: "Put your left foot in. Take your left foot out." After all, fulfilling his desires is "what it's all about."

There's another story in the Bible that is quite different. It is found in the book of Nehemiah. He's my favorite Old Testament character and perhaps the most ordinary man found in all of scripture

He's living as a slave in Persia when he hears that his hometown of Jerusalem is in ruins. The news weighs on him for months, to such an extent that one day his King wonders what's wrong. Upon hearing Nehemiah's concerns, the master allows his servant to return home.

In setting out on the journey, this reluctant man says something so subtle that it could easily be overlooked. Still, in the words of Nehemiah come a key to understanding life in our modern-day world: "I told no one of the work God placed on my heart."

On his heart? Where was the plan to salvage a city? Where were the instructions? Where was the to-do list that he could use to keep track of his progress?

To me, the absence of all the answers turns what this common man did into an act that shows a greater level of obedience than those who were given step-by-step instructions. If the first example was doing the Hokey Pokey, just following God's directions—then Nehemiah had the confidence to get on the dance floor and let his body move to the beat of the music.

Yes, sometimes we have to believe that God will do what He promised. At other moments our faith is best expressed by taking action even when He hasn't promised anything. Having a relationship with God requires us, on occasion, to leave our comfort zone and trust that He will meet up with us somewhere along the journey.

When it comes to my great assignment in life, God remains silent. He has never shared with me his "big picture" vision of what He wants me to do, or the reason why He spared my life. Apparently that remains on a "need to know" basis. Yet He has not failed to place things, people mostly, on my heart. That should be more than enough for now.

Part 9

The Soft-Sell

"Lord, remind me how brief my time on Earth will be. Remind me that my days are numbered and that my life is fleeing away.
(Psalm 39:4 NLT)

Live wisely among those who are not Christians, and make the most of every opportunity.
(Colossians 4:5 NLT)

17

ANOTHER WRECK, A DIFFERENT OUTCOME

On the weekends, it's not unusual to get a call from work. If the interruption comes in the morning, then the conversation is generally quick. On the other hand, when the phone rings in the evening I know some type of crisis is waiting on the other end. The later the call, the more likely it is that I'll be required to head to the office.

When my phone exploded on one particular Saturday night, there was no part of me that wanted to answer it. My son had just gone off to bed, and I was finally enjoying some quiet time. My mind was already rehearsing excuses: left it on vibrate, was asleep and didn't hear it go off, my battery died and the charger is broken.

In the end guilt and responsibility won out. They always do. After four rings I reluctantly picked up. "We just heard from the State Police." The voice of our weekend anchor was trembling with tears. "Karl's dead! He was killed in a motorcycle wreck."

It takes a split second for tragic news to sink in. My brain just didn't comprehend the notion of death right away. That was probably the case because the previous day I was in the company of a healthy person who is now, without explanation, suddenly gone. On Friday Karl was full of life and energy and laughter. How is it possible that just like that, with one phone call, he was wiped away?

Karl was my boss. It was impossible not to like him. Everybody did. He just had a natural zest for life. You'd never guess that he was a few months shy of his sixtieth birthday. His default pace was that of a much younger man; he was always on the go, the type of guy who knew how to be in the "now." I think that's why so many of his younger employees, myself included, truly enjoyed working for this man.

When my mind finally got over the shock, the phone conversation ended in the same manner as so many other weekend interruptions: "Okay, I'm coming in. Let me wake up Brody and we'll be there in a few minutes."

Going into work really didn't make much sense. There was nothing for me to do once I got there. Still, leaving home just felt natural, almost like a reflex. I no longer wanted quiet time for myself. Instead, I so much desired the company of others who shared in the same state of shock and confusion.

I wondered too if any of them were troubled by the same issue that was bothering me. Oh, I dare not be the one to broach the subject. Mentioning it, on this occasion, would be disrespectful and cruel. Someone else would have to bring it up.

You see, Karl made it very clear that he wasn't a believer. He rejected all churches and religions. So walking out of the apartment, with my son asleep in my arms, two questions were on my mind. What did Karl's stance in life mean for his eternal soul? And what did the death of my friend mean for my faith?

HURDLE: GETTING PAST THE PEARLY GATES

Who gets into Heaven? This riddle may be the quintessential question of life.

For some, it all comes down to keeping the Ten Commandments. If they're right, I'm in trouble. One out ten will not get me in. Maybe my score is even lower. Although I've never committed murder, I am guilty of feeling intense hatred. According to Jesus, it's all the same.

Others prefer taking a much larger inventory. They imagine St. Peter holding a ledger of their entire life with all the details, good and bad. He'll let you pass only if the balance tilts towards the positive. Many are drawn to this view because it seems fair. It allows nice people into Heaven. But how does it all add up? There's no way to know. God never provides a formula. Does one plus erase a minus? If the sin is really bad, does it take a collection of good deeds to wipe the slate clean? Lacking the proper math lesson, how does anyone really know where they stand? Would a loving God really use such a vague system?

And then there are the Christians who claim the only way in is through a relationship with Jesus. I resisted this approach for a long time, even after becoming a believer. It seemed so narrow minded. I didn't want to accept Christ just to turn around and condemn others. But in time, something about this notion started to grow on me. This was different from the other theories; it wasn't based on my performance. In fact, in a way, it even went so for to compensate and make up for my lack of perfection. It's like God knew I had no chance of meeting the qualifications on my own, so he sent someone to help cover the gap.

But almost as soon as I came to embrace this way of thinking, something happened. It was something I wasn't prepared for, something that shook me to the core. In short: my faith came in conflict with a face, the pleasant smile of an older man who had treated me so kindly.

You see, there's such a big difference between accepting something in theory and justifying it in reality. How could I explain to others or to myself for that matter, that according to my new beliefs Karl didn't make the cut?

KARL LOVED being the vice president and general manager of a television station. For him the job went far beyond simple business interest. It allowed him to do something on a much larger scale. He really was a community leader. He cared deeply for the city of Wilmington and devoted his time here to make it a better place to live.

Night after night, his calendar was filled with events like the annual Salvation Army dinner. For me, such an occasion was a far cry from my usual night out. But there I was, all the same, sitting directly across from my new boss. It was my first week on the job and Karl wanted to introduce me to the movers and shakers.

As an atheist, not knowing what to do, my eyes glanced down to the floor when the evening started off with a prayer. I wasn't about to join in on the ritual, but at the same time I didn't want to appear disrespectful. Staring at my shoe laces seemed like the only polite alternative.

The chaplain at the podium started off by thanking God for the volunteers, and then for the Salvation Army staff. He made it a point to mention several people by name. Since it was a charitable event, he also needed to pay tribute to all the donors and asked that they be blessed in the year ahead.

He wasn't through yet. He went on and on and on.

He quoted from memory a large section of scripture about looking after the poor and downtrodden. At some point he started to give thanks for the food we were about to eat and hands that prepared it, but my desire to be polite had long since ended. Shoelaces can only hold my attention for so long.

The second my head lifted from the floor and started to look around the room, my eyes bumped directly into Karl's. He was doing the same thing. In fact, I doubt he ever once glanced down, not even to be polite. He was so confident in who he was, so comfortable in his own skin, that he did not need to fake spirituality to impress others. Rolling his eyes at me from across the table he gave me a look as if to say, "Would somebody please wrap this guy up!"

It's easy to like someone when you discover a common bond, but sometimes it takes two people moving in polar opposite directions to really develop respect and love for each other. Karl was a man who had everything in order. His life was the product of a well-devised plan. By comparison, only a month or so after the Salvation Army dinner, everything around me started falling apart.

As my family split up, as I became an emotional wreck at work, for whatever reason Karl stuck with me. He could have written me off as a bad hire, just another drama-plagued employee. But he didn't. The same friendly face that shared a glance with me at a charitable dinner was there to greet me every morning.

He didn't look down on me when I became a churchgoer. He never used words like crutch, or cult. Karl's natural disposition was to offer support, even when it was something he didn't believe in. All that mattered to him was that I had found an outlet, in a brand-new community, to help get through the loneliness.

When he heard I was writing a book on my spiritual journey he demanded to be given a copy, which he actually read. Upon finishing the first version of this manuscript he handed it back, saying: "Now that I know your story, let me tell you mine."

Karl grew up Protestant but left the church as a young adult. "Part of it is still with me, and I think about it from time to time, but I've never gone back. What's the point?" And then he paused for a few seconds, before finishing his thought; "I guess I just never faced the type of crisis where I really needed God."

HURDLE: OPPORTUNITIES LOST

We're all called to share the Gospel, but in our efforts is it possible to do more harm than good? If our approach is too aggressive, can we actually drive seekers in the opposite direction?

It happened to me, when I was an outsider. Believers tried to shove religion down my throat. They seemed to reduce the Cross to a simple insurance policy to get into heaven. It was like they were pitching: "You're in good hands with Jesus." Few actually reflected a loving image of their savior. In fact, their techniques had Him seem hateful and judgmental. When I did finally became a follower it was not because of these people, but rather in spite of them.

There must be a better way.

What would happen if instead of chasing outsiders we created a path for them to travel in our direction? Wouldn't that kind of spiritual reverse psychology be far more effective? All it would take is a commitment to engage in their life, loving them regardless of where they were, sharing with them the sincerity of our faith in good times and bad. If we evangelized in such a way, perhaps the day would come when they would reach out to us.

It all looks good on paper. But as I would tragically discover, through an unwanted phone call on a Saturday night, sometimes time runs out.

KARL'S MEMORIAL SERVICE was an impressive event. It was held in Thalian Hall, Wilmington's landmark Civil War-era theatre.

From my seat in the back of the first level, it was impossible to get a view of either the balcony or top mezzanine floor above me. Based on the parking lot and the overflowing crowd in the lobby, this was a standing-room-only performance.

At least eight people were there to deliver eulogies. The city's chief executive went first. The mayor joked that Karl was a natural-born politician who appeared at every civic and charitable function: "It's a good thing that he never challenged me in an election. I wouldn't have had a chance."

A man from a canine rescue organization appeared on stage with a golden retriever and talked about Karl's heart for animals and all the money he helped raise. A few speakers remembered their friend's impeccable taste in clothing: the pinstriped three-piece suits, the expensive ties, the pocket squares and perfectly polished shoes. About a dozen of Karl's fellow bikers, all wearing leather chaps, occupied a section of seats up front. One of them went to the podium and told us that Karl died "doing what he loved."

No one mentioned God or the concept of Heaven, but it was the only thing on my mind. With each eulogy, it became more and more apparent that the nice man I knew from the office was truly a good guy. He was described as loving, caring, giving, gentle, always there to help the friend in need.

He certainly did that for me, but was I there for him in return? My mind started to replay the one religious conversation the two of us shared. Was there something more I could have said or done? Why didn't I go into more detail about Jesus and what he had really done for us all on the cross? I never even invited Karl to church. Heck, that was the least of my concerns. I never even prayed for the man. It just seemed like his picture-perfect life couldn't benefit from my petitions. Looking back, would any of these things have made a difference?

The last speaker on the stage was the widow. "I want to thank everyone for their nice words, and stories about Karl." She spoke softly, but with that type of strength that only comes out when someone's in mourning. "I've been wondering what he would think of this big production, and all this fuss being made in his honor. And finally, I realized—in fact, there's no doubt in my mind—that he'd be pissed! He'd tell us, 'This wasn't supposed to be my time to go.'"

Her selection of words created one of those awkward but sweet moments when tears and laughter come together in perfect synergy. In fact, there was such a big uproar from the audience that I wondered if anyone else noticed what happened next. As the sound started to fade away, Karl's wife formed her hand into a fist and started to pump it. She was making a gesture meant specifically for her husband. She was telling him "I got you back buddy." As she was getting in this last word, her eyes automatically darted upward toward the ceiling of the theatre and of course to Heaven beyond.

It was clear to me, that in that moment, she believed that Karl was in the company of God. In my seat, just a few feet away, I so desperately wanted to believe it, too.

Confession: I didn't Become a Christian Because I wanted to Get into Heaven

If Christianity was just about a ticket into Heaven, I probably never would have joined the flock. At least not right away. Sure, it sounds like an attractive destination, a lot better than hell, but knowing my finely honed skills of procrastination the conversion would have always been put off until tomorrow.

Instead, my relationship with God was built on something far more immediate. It was no longer possible for me to do it alone. My way wasn't working. I needed a God who was willing to free me from daily burdens and lift problems off my shoulders. I needed the hope that things can work out for good, especially during those moments when it all appears so bad. I needed to believe that it was possible that someone could be aware of all my flaws, know all of my weaknesses, see every blemish and love me still the same.

In short I became a Christian not because what happens in the next world, but because I needed Jesus in this one.

YOU KNOW WHAT REALLY BUGS ME about Karl's death? It's the number of my Christian friends who try to wipe away or discard all my worries and concerns. They tell me that faith is a private matter and that it's impossible for any individual to really know what another is thinking. Some even go so far as to suggest that maybe in the end, Karl finally found Jesus. "You never really know what he was thinking just before he passed" they tell me.

I know they're only trying to comfort me, but something about it just seems rather foolish. And there's no doubt in my mind that it would bother Karl. I can almost hear him: "What are you trying to do? Cover your bets? If you're going to believe in something then believe in it all out. What gives you the right to turn me, in death, into something I never was in life?"

Truth is—and this is hard to swallow—there will never come a time when I like what my faith tells me about my friend. All I know is I am grateful that Karl was in my life.

You see, when I needed it the most, God sent along a man who supported and encouraged me while providing the necessary room to grow. For this assignment, out of infinite wisdom, a man was chosen to help build my faith even though he didn't share in it.

WHAT ABOUT YOU?

1. Who is the Karl in your life? If that person has passed, how do you cope? If the person is living what is the best way for you to share God's love for him/her?

2. What do you think are the qualifications to get into Heaven?

3. What do you think is the best way to share the Gospel?

18

GRADUALLY TO EVANGELISM

There is a guy I know who keeps track of how many people he's "lead to the Lord." To date, by his count, he's helped save twenty-four souls. He's very proud of that number. One day, I am sure, he hopes to break a hundred.

Seems to me there's something wrong with keeping tally. To my friend, successful conversions are not really about bringing people to Christ; instead it's all about improving his own spiritual status. My friend needs the number to see how his faith stacks up. It's a scorecard of sorts. He's beating those Christians who have saved fewer than twenty-four, and trailing those who've converted more.

What's his rate of return? That's the real question. If you're going to make salvation into a competitive sport, then it must be judged not just on score but also on ratio. Hitters have batting averages, quarterbacks have completion rates, and basketball players have field goal percentages. So, I want to know: twenty-four out of how many?

Sure, two dozen sounds like a lot until you watch this guy in action. He approaches at least that many on a daily basis. He doesn't tip waitresses, he leaves Bible tracts. Strangers standing in line at the grocery store are frequently asked if they attend church. Those who share the same elevator with him are given the condensed version of the Gospel. Most of the time, and he admits this, his actions go nowhere. He can go weeks, months, even years without his efforts paying off.

"Well, maybe I planted a seed!"

His defense is typical of people who share in this kind of evangelism, this drive-by Christianity. They like to recite scripture from Isaiah that promises that God's word "will not return in void." (Isaiah 55:11) They believe that good will always, eventually, come from their actions.

If only I could spend my days secretly following my friend around town. The moment his encounter with a stranger ended, I'd be there to offer up apologies on behalf of the entire faith: "We're really not all like that."

Still, as much as his ways annoy me, I have to admit that my own methods are flawed. In fact, my return ratio is equally low. Karl's life—and death—have taught me that.

Herein lies the dilemma of the modern-day church. When it comes to evangelism, we've split up into two camps. We err towards one extreme or the other. Some choose to see every moment and encounter as a chance to throw their seeds. Others want to first cultivate the ground by building relationships. One runs the risk of chasing people away, the other of lost opportunities.

Both sides, of course, have their moments of success. When that happens, when we've helped someone start their walk, we hold up the example and offer it as proof that our approach is the real Christian way.

Did Jesus really approve one style over the other? Maybe not. By preaching and performing miracles in front of thousands, he shared his message in a single instant. By contrast, he built the foundation of his movement on long-term relationships with only a select few.

If Jesus had a message on the right way to evangelize, perhaps it comes during the final moments of his life. His was the center cross, with a thief on either side of Him. From that vantage point, as the story plays out, He shows us all—both sides—how to get in the middle.

So many sermons have been devoted to the one who accepted Christ while dying just a few feet away. When reading of that dramatic moment, you hear the voice of a man who realizes that his own sins and evil deeds have cast this judgment upon him. By comparison, he knows that Jesus has done nothing to deserve the same fate. That's all the cultivation necessary. "I assure you," Jesus tells him, "Today you will be with me in paradise."

With one man down and one to go, the stage seemed perfectly set for another conversion. The other thief must have overheard the guarantee just given out. Jesus loved both men the same but he never turns in the other direction. He says nothing to the second thief. Perhaps in his silence we learn that salvation can never be reduced to a numbers game.

The Lord, from that center position, showed us something all of us have struggled with ever since. He taught us there are times to speak up, and moments when it's best to say nothing.

By remaining silent, towards a man who had just mocked him, Jesus is showing one extreme (the drive-byers) that trying to plant something in hard soil is just a waste of time. And yet, by embracing the first thief, he is teaching those of us in the other extreme something equally important: at some point you do have to throw the seed.

It is my deepest spiritual hope to perfect this balancing act. But my motives are less than pure. Like my friend who keeps a running count, my desire to find the middle ground is far more about me than the people I want to reach.

I just want to avoid going through life haunted by another face, the image of someone I like, and the pain of wondering if perhaps I held on to the seed too long.

PART 10

GRATITUDE

"Enjoy what you have rather than desiring what you don't have. Just dreaming about nice things is meaningless."
(Ecclesiastes 6:9 NLT)

"When you pray, go away by yourself, shut the door behind you, and pray to your father secretly. Then your father, who knows all secrets, will reward you."
(Matthew 6:6 NLT)

19

THE PURSUIT OF GRATITUDE

It didn't matter how many times I turned him down, my pastor friend wasn't going to take "no" for an answer.

For two years, he'd been inviting me to visit his church. I love this man! But there was no way I was going to attend one of his services.

His congregation had a reputation for being on the charismatic side. You know the type of place where people dance in the aisle, where they even talk back to the minister (interrupting his sermon with shouts of "Amen!" "Testify!" and "Preach it!") All of this was way out of my comfort zone. And there was something else too; I didn't like the thought of being the only white guy in an African American Church.

"Oh, my old buddy Doug has never seen me filled with the spirit!"

If I knew my friend was going to draw attention to me, as if I didn't stand out enough on my own, if I knew he was going to make fun of my lack of rhythm and inability to clap on the beat,

I would have continued to turn down his invitation. In truth, his good-natured ribbing was a sign of love. It was almost as if he was telling everybody else; "The white boy is with me."

My long-awaited visit to New Beginnings Church came on the first Sunday in January. "Y'all think this is going to be the best year in your life, don't cha?"

Once on stage, the mild-mannered guy I befriended had disappeared. He was replaced with the type of persona you'd see preaching on public access cable: screaming, strutting back and forth, and using a handkerchief to wipe the sweat off his face. "Let me tell you something; not one of you deserves this year. Not one of you!"

He instructed us to turn to the thirteenth chapter of Luke where we found the story of a fig tree. A vineyard owner had decided to chop it down because after three years it had produced no fruit. "You're that fig tree!" The pastor was yelling at his flock. "Where is your fruit? You spent last year hanging around the wrong crowds, messing around with drugs. Do you have any clue how lucky you are that God didn't get out his ax?"

His style and approach was almost the direct opposite of what I was used to at church. Still, his message hit home, he was speaking to me. Suddenly I was ashamed to have turned down so many of his invitations. Maybe *how* we worship is a lot less important than *Who* we worship

At the end of the story in Luke, an employee talked the vineyard owner into giving the fig tree one more year. As he reached this conclusion, the pastor's tone dramatically softened and I could once again recognize my friend. "What are you going to do with this extra time? What fruit are you going to produce? You need to see this as a gift from God and start from a place of gratitude, giving thanks that He's given you one more year."

In the beginning, my motives were selfish. Becoming a Christian was all about me. My way wasn't working and I needed God to come in and play Mr. Fix It.

Consequently, my earliest prayers were nothing more than cries for help: God, you've got to do this, get me through that, be by my side and show me light at the end of the tunnel.

Perhaps that is the way it's supposed to be. If not for crisis mode, many of us would lack the incentive to start the journey. But the chaos eventually fades and we arrive at a spiritual right of passage. We find ourselves spending time with God, not for what he can do for us, but simply because of who He is.

For me, the transition happened one night in January while I was literally down on my knees.

JOURNALING, even reading the Bible, has become natural to me, but my traditional prayer life has always been a struggle. Talking to God just feels so awkward.

Maybe the problem is a simple case of stage fright. There's this internal pressure not to say the wrong thing or mess up my lines. I want to sound smart, eloquent and profound; so why do I feel like a rambling idiot? Half the time I don't even know how to start. "Heavenly Father, Abba Father, Lord Almighty, Creator of Heaven and Earth. You are a kind and merciful God."

By the time all that is out of my mouth some noise in the apartment—the squeaking of pipes, the ticking of a clock, the neighbors fighting on the other side of the paper thin walls—has already distracted me. And so I feel the urge to start over from scratch. "Heavenly Father, Abba Father, Lord Almighty…"

Something, actually everything, was different that Sunday night following the service at New Beginnings Church. The sermon was so inspiring, the notion of gratitude so overwhelming, that I just wanted to follow my friend's advice and "give thanks."

I vividly remember kneeling on the side of my bed (just like my parents taught me) and folding my hands together with overlapping fingers. While I stayed on my knees for the entire prayer, the position of my hands didn't last. Not long after getting started my posture changed. My arms opened up as if I was going to catch something falling from above.

"I just want to give You thanks for everything You've done for me." It was a strange way to start. What happened to all the glorious titles and superfluous names? Where was the fear of offending Him? Is it okay to just jump into a prayer like that?

Much of what I said to God was actually spoken out loud, but not all of it. There were several moments when I just shared my thoughts with Him. Maybe words aren't necessary to profoundly speak to God.

I thought of the sermon from a few hours earlier and the notion that I had given God every reason to take out his ax. That reminded me of being hit by the semi truck. A year had already passed since the wreck, but for the first time it really did seem like a second chance, and there on my knees, I was grateful for it.

On the surface, not much had changed about my circumstances since becoming a Christian. But losing myself in prayer took me to a deeper place where I could see some of the work going on inside of me. Whatever happened to that nervous guy who sweated the small stuff and was once prescribed anxiety medication? Where was the roller-coaster ride that constantly took me from a high point down to a lonely valley? When did things start leveling off? Should a missing-persons report be filed on that guy who was always searching for love? Where did he go? There was no woman in my life, there wasn't even a prospect, but in that moment I knew that love was all around me.

I gave thanks for my son, and for all the joy and laughter that comes with being a father. Did God really understand whom He had chosen to play this part? How unqualified was I to be a role model and a spiritual influence to anyone, let alone a little boy? But instead of feeling overwhelmed by this, I focused on the fact that He placed his trust in me and gave thanks for that too.

Something else had quietly changed over time. Two years earlier, I was worried about losing custody and the love of a child. And now: "The most important relationship in my life is the one I have with You." I know that part of the prayer was spoken out loud because the sound of the words scared me. What if God took that as an invitation to test me, to allow something to happen to my son? So I quickly added: "Please look after Brody and let him always feel the love of the Father, especially during those times when his dad can't be around."

There was so much else to give thanks for: my parents, my siblings, old friends, new friends. My mind was quickly filling up with the names of all these people who stuck by me and invested in me. This list was taking me far beyond a place of gratitude; this was now about being truly blessed.

Normally, eventually, if I ever got there, my prayers would end with a list of things I hoped God would rescue me from: my financial problems, getting me out of the shoebox-sized apartment meant for a college kid (not a man in his thirties,) my loneliness, my fear.

On that night, none of it was mentioned. Not in words, not in thought. It was strange, but I was now giving God "thanks" for things that had not yet even happened: "I know that this is not my final stop, that there's more in store for me, things that I can't even fathom right now. I am so overwhelmed by how You are using me, and so excited to see how it all comes out. Mostly

I am anxious to meet the person you're already modeling me into. I have a feeling that I'm really going to like that guy."

More than twenty minutes had passed on my knees. It seemed like it lasted only a few seconds. During that time I am sure there were noises and potential distractions, but they all went unnoticed. This evening was just about a man whose spiritual life was taking the next step forward. "I don't deserve all You have done, and all You are about to do, but I am truly grateful that You are my God! And I pray this in Your Son's name, my glorious savior: Jesus Christ. Amen!"

HURDLE: CO-INKY DINK

A small, but significant, difference between a person of a faith and a nonbeliever comes in the value that each of us places in the most bizarre moments of our lives. I am talking about those situations when everything just magically comes together, when time and space collide with perfect precision. Christians do not have a monopoly on such quirky events. Everyone has experienced them.

The contrast comes in what we give credit for causing the harmony. The outsider writes it all off as random luck or coincidence, maybe they say its Karma.. The follower, on the other hand, will experience a similar occasion and choose to see God's hands in action.

ONLY A FEW HOURS after the prayer, as soon as I walked into the office the following morning, a coworker motioned me over. He was going through a financial dilemma. He had just gotten married, moved into his wife's place and put his bachelor condo up for sale.

His timing couldn't have been worse. The housing market had recently come crashing down. Six months into his marriage, not only had he received no offers, but no potential buyers had even looked or walked through his old place.

"I've got to do something about it." He told me that morning at work. "And I've been thinking about you."

He knew all about my situation. He knew that I hated my apartment. He knew that my ex hated it more. In our initial custody battle, she tried to limit my time with our son because he didn't have a room of his own. Fortunately the judge said no. All the same, I wanted to get out of there.

"The thing is, I can't rent it out to just anybody. It's filled with all my stuff. My wife already had a washer, dryer, refrigerator, all the furniture. So I just left it all there instead of putting it in storage."

Before he made the official offer, I already knew where he was going. It seemed so surreal. For several months I had tried to take the issue into my own hands. I had looked around at duplexes and townhomes but the math never worked out. Even when it seemed possible to pay a little more in rent, there was always the threat of going further into debt. My credit cards would get an instant workout buying all the things that were lost in the breakup

And now everything was being taken care of like magic. Why was it all coming together? What did I do to deserve this? Did my prayer from the previous night have anything to do with me getting a new place to live? Christians always talk about surrender. Is that what I did when I was down on my knees?

"It's a three-bedroom. That's maybe more room than you need, but one of them is set up as an office, with a huge desk. It would be perfect for your writing."

The mortgage payments he wanted me to make were actually less than I was already paying in rent. When I accepted his terms, he acted as if he was the one receiving the favor. I guess sometimes gratitude can be a two-way street.

There is no doubt in my heart that this is a case of spiritual cause and effect. I believe, just have faith, that my prayer somehow got things in motion. At least that's what the "New Doug" thinks.

You see, the "Old Doug" was there too. He's tried to downplay it all. He focuses on the details and leans on reason: "Come on! Do you remember what you said in the prayer? You never asked for anything specifically. It's not like you said: 'Hey, give me a new place to live' and BOOM there was a new place to live. Don't get carried away here."

But I choose to get carried away. In the end, faith comes down to a choice and I've made mine. Without any means of proving it—even lacking the ability to turn off that part of my mind that wants to talk me out of it—to me these quirky events are the ultimate sign that God is in control. And proof that if we're willing to let go, He'll guide us where He wants us to be.

Something my friend said, when we shook hands to seal the deal, only confirms all this in my mind: "I've been meaning to talk to you for a while about this, and when I woke up this morning I knew today had to be the day."

CONFESSION: I'VE TRIED TO SEDUCE GOD.

What happened to me was much bigger than getting a new place to live. It felt as if the secret to God had finally been revealed. I had figured Him out, virtually all on my own, how He operates, how He responds and what He expects. Now that I had the key, I could use it to get everything I ever wanted.

It was just a matter of acting grateful. So night after night, a little game of seduction played out. I tried to duplicate all the moves that had already proven successful. I'd kneel at the same spot against my bed, try to say virtually the exact same words. If it worked once surely it would work again.

It never did.

Looking back, I'm embarrassed to have been so foolish. I was like a husband who turned on some music and asked his wife to dance in the living room. He did it for no other reason but to make her smile. Later the two of them shared a romantic night. Now, motivated by something totally different, every time she walks into the room the stereo instantly starts playing her favorite song. With the first beat she knows exactly what he's really after.

To be sure, gratitude is important to God. He is most pleased with us when we are pleased with Him, but that is something you cannot fake nor manipulate. Gratitude doesn't count for anything unless it's genuine and our motives are pure.

A BIG GOAL for many Christians is to live a life in constant communion with God. The vision comes from something Paul wrote in the fifth chapter of 1 Thessalonians: "Pray continually," or ceaselessly or without stopping, depending on the version.

That sounds great, but is it really possible to do that: to be connected with God, every waking moment of the day?

"Sure it's possible," friends told me early on in my walk. "You're always thinking, aren't you? Well, instead of thinking to yourself, you direct those thoughts up to Heaven."

And so I started a habit that was supposed to make me more spiritual. God's name was casually dropped into the most routine and mundane thoughts, as if that alone would bring me closer to Him. The alarm clock would go off in the morning and it became "God, let me have a few more minutes of sleep." At the supermarket I'd ask for His advice. "What do you think God? Should I get crunchy or smooth peanut butter?" Even when my thoughts were impure, I tried to make them holier by bringing him into the mix. "God, look at that woman over there. She is hot!"

All of that came to a sudden stop when I focused on the next line of scripture that Paul wrote. "Pray continually," and then he added "Give thanks in all circumstances, for this is God's will for you in Christ Jesus."

When you take those two lines together the key concept is not just constant communion, but constant gratitude.

Now when the alarm clock goes off, I try to give thanks for a good night's sleep and for having something to wake up for. At the grocery store, the gratitude is for having a choice. Not everyone in this world gets to pick what kind of food they'll eat and I do. (How can you not be thankful for that?) When I see an attractive woman, I'm now appreciative that God formed the two genders so differently.

It's not like I do this with every thought or in every moment of the day—far from it. But I'm okay with that. These days I am far more concerned with *how* I pray to God than *how often* I pray to Him.

WHAT ABOUT YOU?

1. Make a gratitude list; include people, circumstances and character traits.

2. What strange moment has happened in your life for which you choose to give God the credit? Explain.

3. In what ways have you tried to manipulate or seduce God? How did it work out?

20

GRADUALLY TO THANKSGIVING

It was the evening before my father's visit. We hadn't seen each other for at least six months...and we weren't going to see a lot of each other now. Dad's last-minute vacation didn't give me enough notice to take the week off. "That's okay," he reassured me. "You go to work and I'll hang out with the grandson."

His kind words aside, it was impossible not to feel bad. What kind of son lets his father travel across the country only to desert him once he arrives? So, I turned to God for help: "Please let me be able to get away from work, at least for a little bit, while dad is in town."

It was a pretty straightforward prayer, succinct, right to the point. And it certainly felt like what I was asking for was in no way against God's will. But biblically speaking was there something wrong about the way I approached Him?

James, the half-brother of Jesus, warned us about how we pray. "You want something but don't get it," he starts off the fourth chapter of the book that bears his name. "You do not have, because you do not ask God. When you ask, you do not receive, because you ask with wrong motives."

Motives? My motives were pure! I just wanted to spend more time with my father. But, as I would painfully discover, only a few hours after his plane landed, something was a little bit off.

The new perspective literally came from my gut. You see, at three o'clock in the morning, the world's most excruciating pain shot me straight out of bed. Okay, like many men, I tend to be on the melodramatic side when it comes to physical pain. But this time it was sincerely bad. Short of a gun-shot wound, or a knife to the abdomen, I didn't know how it was possible for a human being to hurt this much. My stomach was on fire!

Dad was sleeping in a bedroom down the hall. He had spent the previous day on airplanes and in rental cars. I didn't want to wake him up. The pain would pass on its own. Wouldn't it? Maybe aspirin would help, maybe stretching, maybe walking around, sitting down, going to the bathroom, throwing up. None of it worked. Oh, every so often I'd find just the right position: with my feet propped up or my head between my legs, for a split second there'd be comfort and relief. And then "OUCH!" The pain would come back with vengeance!

It was a kidney stone.

My dad knew it right away. He diagnosed it as soon as I woke him up. He told me they run in the family. He even tried to make a joke that they're "*passed* from one generation to the next."

That's exactly what you want when you're hurting, an old man making puns.

Moments later at the hospital, waiting for my turn in the emergency room, I found myself in the fetal position. That wouldn't have been so bad if I weren't lying on the bathroom floor. Sometimes desperate men do desperate things.

Who knows why, but in that time and place, my mind started to think about the prayer from the previous night. Suddenly it was all so clear. James was right: there was something wrong with my motives. My request didn't come from a source of gratitude. To be honest, it was driven by guilt.

I failed to give thanks that my dad was making the trip in the first place. Yes, we'd only have limited time together, but his being here was still a huge gift. Why did I let my obligations overwhelm me? The more I thought about it, the more my prayer appeared to be nothing more than just asking God to put me in two places at once. How could that possibly be in His will?

So with the view of the world that only comes when you hit rock bottom (a bathroom floor is about as low as you can get,) I sincerely wanted another chance.

There was just one thing: how do you show gratitude when you're in so much pain that there's almost nothing to be thankful for? And so, I began the most insincere prayer ever muttered in the history of the world. Virtually every sentence was interrupted with cries of agony: "Heavenly Father, you are a merciful God. OH, PLEASE MAKE IT STOP! I trust you, Lord, and know that you have placed me in the perfect position." Honestly those words came out of my mouth even though my head was lying on a surface undoubtedly covered in urine. "Thank you for bringing dad down here. I know the two of us will have a great time together Wow! Man! I THINK THE BABY'S COMING!"

I never even got to finish the prayer. My father suddenly opened the men's room door. One of the nurses was finally calling me back.

As I struggled to get to my feet, I discovered my stomach wasn't the only thing pounding inside of me. That sledge hammer feeling was back with tremendous force. This may sound strange, but this time it actually came in the sound of chuckling. I really think God was having fun at my expense.

At first I thought He was laughing at me, but when He let me in on the joke I instantly enjoyed his sense of humor and laughed alongside Him. "Well," he told me as I walked out the door, "At least you'll have tomorrow off to spend some time with your dad."

PART 11

MINISTRY

"I will bless you and make you a blessing to others." (Genesis 12:2 NLT)

"You are generous because of your faith. And I am praying that you will really put your generosity to work, for in so doing you will come to an understanding of all the good things we can do for Christ." (Philemon :6 NLT)

21

The Sign

You ever notice that when people talk about getting a sign from God it's almost always a story of Him saying yes?

We all know someone who has rushed into romance because they believed that the budding relationship was divine intervention. How do you argue with such logic? "We drive the same kind of car. We were born in the same hospital. Our mothers have the same first name—I think God's telling me this is Mr. Right."

All of us seek confirmation. We come up with the game plan and then expect God to sign off on it. If we hear nothing, if it feels like He's rejected our course, we keep twisting and turning the proposal, overlooking all the negative side effects, until we find some solid ground to make a moral stance. Few people want to move forward without God, even if that means creating a situation where we fool ourselves into thinking that He is on board.

Maybe the problem is that we look for the wrong kind of guidance. I firmly believe that God has sent me signs, but never to get me to do what I already wanted to do in the first place. What would be the point in that? Instead he's given me signals to move when I've been reluctant, to get me in gear, to go ahead with something that I've been putting off or even dreading.

This book is a result of such signs.

The notion to write first came from my pastor. He told me: "Put your story on paper. You never know who it may help."

He needed to be more specific. He didn't make it clear that he was only expecting a few pages.

And so, totally naive, I went to work on an outline that quickly got out of hand. How could I talk about coming back to God, without also describing the details behind leaving him in the first place? Should I expose all the pain and mistakes of my life? What about all the characters. This wasn't just my story, others were involved. I'd have to introduce them all: Chisel, my son, my ex, the stranger at the swimming pool who recommended his church, the all-American couple who cried on the picnic table, Richie the former beer distributor and all the others who supported me along the way.

After just a few minutes of scribbling notes, the project was already being shelved. This was not something that could be knocked out in a few days. It would take much longer. I didn't have that kind of time.

Plus I didn't have the room. My shoe box-sized apartment had no work station, no desk, no place to actually invest the energy required by the project. "Maybe some day," I kidded myself.

And so I walked away from it all, literally. I threw the notes in the garbage, only to realize that the trashcan was already filled. I grabbed the bag and walked to the dumpster shared by the entire complex. There, on the outside of the huge green bin, was a small desk and swivel chair. Both were in good condition and now up for grabs, the kind of thing renters place aside when their lease is up.

It was impossible to look at the discovery without reliving the scene that had just taken place inside the apartment. Suddenly that internal voice was testing me: “So, what’s your excuse now?”

I grabbed the notes out of the trash-bag and walked home. After nightfall, when the coast was clear, I returned to the dumpster to get the goods.

HURDLE: SHHH! QUIET!

There's a website that promises to figure out your calling. You log on, look over twenty-plus statements like "I am able to convey the Gospel in ways that people can understand," or "I am compelled to learn everything about the Bible."

Using a dropdown bar, you vote on what degree the sentence applies to your life: "All the time, Some of the time, Occasionally, or None of the time." Finish the questionnaire and just click on a button. A few seconds later the results are broken down.

Obviously, I am a little skeptical. There is no way a computer program can determine God’s will for your life. Besides, even if it were a hundred percent accurate, it kind of misses the point. The big question isn’t “God, what do you want me to do?” It’s really “God, who do you want me to be?”

WRITING IS A PAIN.

It didn’t matter how much I thought about a chapter, outlined it, researched it, talked it over with friends. When it came time to do the work, my mind was always as blank as the sheet of paper. *Why would God give me something so hard and complicated? Doesn’t He have anything easier?*

Writing, in and of itself, is not a ministry. You're not engaging with other people, forming relationships, and building community with them. You're just sitting by yourself, sometimes for hours, with only your thoughts as company. For me the project wasn't a calling. Instead it was something far more important. It was a way for me to have one-on-one time with God.

That's what kept me from quitting. That realization gave me a huge sense of freedom. The intimidation of getting started came from the notion that someday people may read what I put down. When I had an audience of only one, even though that one was the creator of Heaven and Earth, the pressure to be perfect was gone and in its place I found communion. You can't establish roots without it.

Maybe your pastor delivers a sermon on Sunday morning that replenishes the soul. Perhaps in the middle of the week you attend a small group where friends hold you accountable. But in the end, it's the alone time that takes the spiritual relationship to entirely new levels.

Working on the book forced me to face the past, both recent and distant. And even though this was still my story, for the first time I was seeing the role that God played in it. His was more than just a cameo appearance. He was always there—always with me—especially during those times when I was not with Him.

There was even something refreshing about the more painful moments. Reliving them revealed one of God's most beautiful character traits. He is a redeemer who won't let anything go to waste—even those uglier moments. There was a purpose for them. They weren't baggage. They were part of the journey, too. And now it felt like He was eager to cash them in and put them to use for the benefit of His kingdom.

Some Christians have a name for this type of one-on-one atmosphere. They call it quiet time. For me there was nothing quiet about it at all. There was the constant clacking away of a keyboard, the thud of a racquet ball bouncing off the wall (I always have a ball close at hand when I write.) There was even the sound of me verbally asking questions of God and then shouts of praise when it felt like He was revealing something new.

More than just a book was taking form. As the work went on, it became clear that I was being molded and shaped, too. With each page the roots grew deeper, with each chapter the faith became more stable.

I started a project hoping it would help people change. By the time it was finished I realized that its purpose all along—God's purpose for it– was that it would help me to change. Because each time you go searching for God, you eventually end up finding yourself.

I was now able to look beyond myself to others.

HURDLE: REACHING BACK

There's a line in scripture that perhaps answers the riddle behind the meaning of life. It's a rather obscure sentence. It's seldom quoted and rarely talked about. In fact when most believers get to it in the Bible, because it's sandwiched between far more famous verses, they probably read right over it. And yet these few words provide so much hope and purpose.

It is found in the story of Abraham. After making the unconventional selection of a man in his seventies to start a religious movement, God offers a promise. If Abraham agrees to leave his home and go to a foreign land, God will make his name famous and turn his family into a great nation.

You've heard that part of the story before, but it's what said next that is too often overlooked. God basically tells Abraham that if he does these things: "I will bless you" and then adds the crucial one line: "I will make you a blessing to others."

The promise of fame and historic importance is made to Abraham alone; it does not have any direct implication to our life. But I truly believe that the second part is offered to everyone who is willing to follow God.

We are all capable of being a blessing. If we do what He wants, become the person He desires for us to be, then our paths will cross, at the precise moment and time, with those who need us.

WHO DO YOU THINK is the most effective at ministering to someone on drugs? I'd point towards an individual who's successfully battled an addiction of their own. I'd also venture to guess that a married person does a far better job providing Christian-based counseling to a troubled couple than someone who is single.

Yes, there are exceptions to this theory. But in most cases people confide in someone who can relate to their trials and tribulations. They need to be told: "Take my hand. I've been in this same hole before and I know the way out."

Two years into my walk, an opportunity presented itself. The church was in need of a facilitator for the weekly Starting Point class. Perhaps more than anything the course is what changed my life, or at least my way of looking at life.

Shortly after attending my first service, I enrolled in the ten-week program. It was a place for me to ask questions, to express my doubt and to engage others in debate. It's also where I met

Richie, the former beer distributor, and learned for the first time that Christians can express love without trying to change you.

Only two short years later and I was being asked to turn around and reach back, to help others make their first few steps in the walk.

Earlier I told you about the former party girl who eventually went off to the seminary. She was in a Starting Point class of mine. I got to see her life transform, but she's not the only one. Each group has had an example like that.

There've been those who walked through the door after walking out of prison: breaking and entering, credit card fraud, one session had three individuals (all strangers to each other) who had a history in counterfeiting. Many joined after facing a personal tragedy, be it the murder of a father or the death of a friend in a car wreck. There's also been financial problems, family issues, eating disorders, sexual abuse, gambling addictions, extreme loneliness and those who talked about suicide.

It's always a room filled with broken people—and I am one of them. Once upon a time, in the not-too-distant history, I would have looked down and avoided some of those who showed up. But it's impossible to judge others when you've become painfully aware of your own human weaknesses.

My role is to keep the discussion on topic. I'm also there to provide biblical perspective for any questions that should arise. Although the truth is people are seldom looking for answers. They just want to be heard. They want to be understood. Other than occasionally stealing a line from Richie, "A few years ago I used to wonder the same thing, too," my main job is simply to listen.

In return, I've been granted a front-row seat to the most spectacular show on Earth. From that vantage point I've seen the levels God is willing to go to reach an individual. And once

He gets them, firmly in His Grasp, I watch first-hand the unfolding of the slow and methodical process of restoring hope.

When the ten weeks are up, no matter how much growth and change may have occurred, at the end of the last session, I always leave knowing that I got more out of the group than anyone else.

That's the magic of faith. It's the only commodity where the more you give away, the more you actually end up having. In fact, in order to really understand what you believe you first have to start sharing it with others.

CONFESSION: I NEED PRAISE

The moment each chapter was finished, I'd always print a few copies out and give them to a select group of friends. Their feedback was important. They told me what needed tweaking and gave me advice on how to make it better.

While I benefited from their criticisms, it was the kudos that really meant the most. I needed to hear that the work had promise that I was on to something, that it was bordering on brilliance.

The same was true of Starting Point. Anytime we had a really good discussion, I'd cling to the comments about how much people were getting out of the group.

I am torn on this issue. On one hand, the positive reinforcement was necessary to keep me going. Without it, I would have failed to accomplish what it felt like God was calling me to do.

On the other hand, by taking credit and basking in the praise, I knew that I was really deflecting the glory off of Him and on to me.

MY PASTOR allowed me to make a brief presentation to his staff. The book was done and I wanted to give the first copies to all those who worked for the church.

Many of them had become friends, others remained strangers. And yet, because of their dedication, they were all part of my story. They belonged to an organization that was really touching people and changing lives.

At the end of the speech, I took the pink sheet of paper that was once created at a business retreat and presented it to Richie. As he took the frame from my hand, a single tear trickled down his cheek. His colleagues instantly stood up and cheered.

The applause was a nice touch, but I wanted them to be louder. I needed more noise! It was my only hope of drowning out the nagging voice convicting me from the inside. "What are you doing here? You know the work's not finished yet."

WHAT ABOUT YOU?

1. What kind of signs have you gotten from God? How do you know they came from Him and not of your own creation?

2. What does your quiet time look like?

3. What are you doing to reach back to others? Name a few people to whom you could be a blessing.

22

GRADUALLY TO PATIENCE

There's a story in the Gospels that totally frustrates me. It gets under my skin because it doesn't make any sense. It's so bizarre, so nonsensical, so out there, that it's impossible for me to read without getting a little angry.

It all takes place during those forty days in the desert when Jesus is tempted by Satan. The devil goes after him with food and the offer of an earthly kingdom. That part I understand. Jesus has been fasting for a long time so he had to be hungry and many have fallen to the allure of riches or material goods.

My problem is with the other temptation. The Bible says that Satan takes Jesus to the highest point of the Temple and tells him: "Jump!"

Am I missing something here? What's tempting about that? It couldn't have taken a lot of will power to turn down the request. The modern day equivalent would be someone telling you to stand in the middle of traffic. What happened on that rooftop seems more like a bad game of "Dare."

Oh, I know where the enemy is coming from. His strategy is pretty clear. He is either trying to kill Jesus off or just get him to test God. Either way, he separates the son from the father. But an offer of leaping off a building and plummeting to the ground below, why would he even think that would work?

I finally got it!

It took years of processing those few lines of scripture, but I now know what Satan was up to. The truth wasn't revealed to me in reading. A light never went off. Instead, for me to understand the temptation, how powerful it was, I first had to fall into the trap myself.

You see, when the earlier version of this book was done, both mind and body knew that it wasn't completely finished. I was even convicted on the matter. This guilty, nagging feeling was constantly with me. There were certain things that I was supposed to change. God let me know that He didn't like the ending, and He started to burden me with this vision of closing out each chapter with an essay.

It was just too much work. I'd already spent several months on the project. I was tapped out. The time had come to move on to something else. No one would ever know that I had cut corners. The book was good enough. Good enough to print out and give to friends, good enough to get a literary agent to represent it, good enough to send out to publishing houses. And good enough to earn a collection of rejection letters.

In rushing to completion, in doing it my way, I was really taking a jump from the top of the temple.

That's what the Devil was up to, that's why he thought his plan actually had a chance. Satan's strategy was telling Jesus that angels would catch him, carrying him gently to the ground. That hook had nothing to do with saving his life. Instead it was about creating a spectacle. He was telling Jesus: "Everyone down there is going to see this happen. They're going to watch you float to the bottom. They're going to recognize that you are who you claim to be! This is ingenious! You can accomplish three years of work in just three seconds. All you have to do is jump! Just jump!"

The pressure must have been overwhelming! If only for a split second, Jesus had to think about everything he could avoid. He wouldn't have to deal with the egos of John and James, the denial of Peter or the betrayal of Judas. He could escape the rejection in His hometown of Nazareth and all the headaches caused by the Pharisees. Perhaps He could also get out of that painful death on the Cross and the burden of taking on the sins of the world.

When I think of the temple in those terms, when I try to hold on to a sense of his humanity, it really is amazing to me that Jesus had the strength to stay still. He not only was ready to answer his calling, but he had the will to do it God's way. By not taking things into his own hands, he shows us that sometimes the hardest leap of faith is when you leave your feet exactly where they are.

And Satan showed us something too. The enemy revealed one of his favorite tricks. Perhaps he wasn't trying to kill Jesus. To be successful he didn't need such extremes. He just had to throw things off a degree or two. All he was after was one moment when Jesus failed to surrender. If that happened, our savior would lack the qualifications to be the Lamb of God.

He probably uses the same tactics on the rest of us. Maybe he's already given up hope that you'll completely avoid your calling. He's now willing to settle for some cut corners and the easy way out. A victory for him is when good enough becomes good enough.

The funny thing is, in my case, after jumping into this book, God did allow me to float gently to the bottom. His loving hands protected me. Other than a few bumps and bruises to my ego, the journey down was painless.

Once there, on the ground, He refused to let go. He wasted no time in pointing back to the top, and telling me this time we needed to try it His way.

PART 12

PEACE

"What I've always feared has
happened to me. What I dreaded
has come to be. I have no peace,
no quietness, I have no rest; instead
only trouble comes."
(Job 3:25-26 NLT)

"But when you are praying,
first forgive anyone you are
holding a grudge against, so
that your Father in heaven
will forgive your sins, too."
(Mark 11:25 NLT)

23

When Faith Meets Fear

The distance between Wilmington and the small town of Benson, North Carolina, is exactly ninety-two miles. I know each one of them intimately. The interstate connecting the two runs through undeveloped farmland, offering little in sight-seeing, but everything along the route is familiar to me.

I've made the trip, several times a month, for four years now. And then I get where I'm going, and after only twenty minutes or so, it's time to turn right back around and head home again.

There's always a sense of adventure to it. In large part that's due to the excitement of seeing my son. Other times the thrill is directly attributed to the fear that my vehicle may not make it. There was the one occasion when my front tire exploded, and on another trip the head gasket blew out. Even when everything is in proper working order, the last few miles are always filled with a sense of nervousness. The moment my car exits the highway and starts navigating around the small town, I begin to worry about what kind of drama may greet me. For the most part the encounters have been non-eventful, but you never know when dealing with an ex.

The story of how she wound up in this rural community is a long and complicated one. When we first moved to North Carolina, one of her distant relatives offered a vacant home there for just a few months during the transition. After the breakup, my ex decided to stay put.

As part of our joint-custody agreement, it fell on me to provide the shuttle service. And so I've traveled the road in pouring-down rain and when temperatures were so hot that skin and upholstery became one. The trip followed both good and bad days at work, with the distance providing time either to stress over some problem or to pat myself on the back for a job well done. It seemed to always be made when the budget was tight and gas was at record highs, although looking back there were plenty of times when money was no issue. Sometimes a conversation with a friend or listening to a new CD made the miles go by a little bit quicker, but it was always a tiresome haul.

And now, on a Friday in February, it was time to make the journey again. I had left work early and if things worked out perfectly, it would be possible to get there and back before night fall.

The gas tank was full, the sun was shining and there was nothing plaguing my mind. Nothing, that is, until my phone buzzed with a text message: "Don't bother coming," my ex crudely told me. "We're in Louisiana."

HURDLE: FALLING DOMINOES

"Faith" is a bizarre word. How we use it, what we mean by it, greatly depends on where we are in our walks. The word refuses to be stagnant. There's life to It;, it's always moving and evolving.

For most of my adult life, the term was used simply to describe one's feelings about God. Those who believed in him had faith. Those who didn't lacked it.

To the follower, the word takes on a slightly different meaning. It's about a response: "taking a leap of faith," or "an act of faith," or "stepping out in faith."

Finding such courage means the word has to change again. This time the focus is on us. Wondering if there's a God or what He wants us to do gets replaced with the scariest question of them all. Now we look to the Heavens and ask: "Did I really hear you correctly?"

THE TEXT MESSAGE didn't say a lot. It didn't need to. It already told me more than I wanted to know; my ex had broken the joint-custody agreement and moved our son across several state lines. Later she'd tell me that it was just a temporary thing, but I knew there was no intention of returning.

This was my worst fear coming true. I prayed about this exact thing and asked God's protection at least a thousand times before. On so many occasions it felt like He responded. That sledgehammer sensation was there to reassure me. "I didn't make you a father," the Spirit told me on one particular night, "just to separate you from your son."

I believed in those words. They got me through the hard times. Like when I had to tell my son "no" after dropping him off at his mother's house. (Sometimes as an infant he'd chase after me with diaper bag in hand demanding to come along.)

Later, when he was old enough to talk on the phone, those words helped ease the pain that comes along with hearing the voice of a child say, "I miss you daddy." And in the last year they allowed me to face the dreaded deadline of full-time school and the knowledge that eventually something would have to change with our 50/50 arrangement. The promise told me there was no need to worry, that somehow it would all work itself out.

But now, as I tried to apply the words to the latest, unwanted development, the very sentence that once gave me comfort was mocking me.

None of this changed my belief in God. So much growth and development had occurred that it would be impossible to ever again debate His existence. Instead of doubting God, I doubted myself: specifically my ability to hear His voice and to discern His will for my life.

Did I miss something? Did I get it wrong? Did that promise have anything do with God at all, or was it something I invented? Was it just wishful thinking, or a defense mechanism, or my subconscious at work? And if I did misinterpret something, on an issue as important as this one, how could I ever trust that sledgehammer feeling again?

My faith had suddenly turned into a fragile row of dominoes. As the first piece toppled over, I had to wonder if any of the others would remain standing.

HURDLE: PICKING SIDES

One of the most vivid memories from my childhood took place in the early winter of 1984. The men of the Wahl family got together to watch an NFL play-off game on television.

No one gave our hometown Detroit Lions much of a chance. But somehow, with the clock ticking down, our boys were in a position to pull off a major upset.

I don't remember who they were playing, but I'll never forget what happened next. As the field goal unit came out, with only a few seconds left, the television set cut to a close-up of our head coach. He was standing on the sidelines with his eyes closed and hands folded over in front of his mouth. He was praying—I guess asking God for a winning kick.

The cameras went back to the action just in time to see the play. The snap went off, the hold went down, the ball went up.... and to the right—the wide right. The game was over. The Lions had lost.

Why did God ignore the prayer of our coach? It was a profound question for an eleven-year-old boy. Of course it never occurred to me that other people, including the players and fans of the opposite team, (let alone every bookie in America), may have been praying, too, and asking for something completely different.

A MONTH had come and gone without any sign of my son. Lawyers were hired, motions were filed, and the battle lines were drawn. I was insisting he be brought back to North Carolina. My ex wanted him to stay in Louisiana.

Night after night I turned to God in prayer hoping for some confirmation. If only He'd provide assurance that I'd heard the promise correctly, somehow I'd make it through. But it never came.

Shortly after starting one prayer a strange question formed in my mind: "What do you think she's praying for right now?" It was very subtle, hardly the sledgehammer sensation I'd experienced before. Although, at that point, my confidence was blown to such an extent that nothing would have appeared to be from God. Besides, my ex didn't pray….or did she?

She calls herself a Christian. I've even heard her talk about the Cross and the importance of having a Savior. But she doesn't attend church on a regular basis, never reads the Bible and doesn't exactly hang out with a group of followers.

All the same, a vision was forming in my head. My mind was drawing a picture of my ex in deep prayer. I could see her. It looked real—too real. She was on her knees asking for the exact opposite of everything I wanted. Suddenly I was afraid. What if God listened to her and not me?

The mental image forced me to look at the conflict from a totally different point of view—from her point of view. For my ex, Louisiana was the Promised Land, the place where everything would start coming together. It's where life would be easier. She knew I'd oppose the move, but in her mind God couldn't possibly be against it.

The more I thought about her phantom prayer, the less evil she appeared. She started to lose the image of an enemy, or someone who launched a sinister plan of attack. She was now vulnerable, misguided, someone who needed compassion, someone very human.

I hated this new way of looking at things

This was a time for some Old Testament wrath. Throw down a lightning bolt. Send down a plague of locusts or frogs! At least find her in contempt of court and let the judge rule in my favor.

Every part of my body was crying out for justice, for the wrong to be righted, for the guilty to be punished, but God was pushing me in a totally different direction, a place where I didn't want to go. It wasn't enough that my son was already gone, now God was trying to take away my anger, too.

At least, that's what I think He was doing.

CONFESSION: THE ENEMY HAD A HOLD ON ME

When people talk about "the enemy," it always makes me feel uncomfortable. Oh, I know in the last chapter there was a reference to Satan, but even writing that didn't come naturally for me.

The problem is that too often believers use the "dark side" as a convenient excuse, or a way for them to pass the buck on their own bad decisions and stupid mistakes. Nothing makes me madder than seeing a Christian exposed in scandal: infidelity in their marriage, an addiction to drugs, corruption at the office, only to have them turn around and try to wipe it away with a simple; "The devil made me do it."

Still, you have to acknowledge that the enemy is real. He's part of the spiritual landscape, comes with the package. If I believe in God, then it's also required to believe in Satan.

He still doesn't deserve the blame for my situation or circumstances. Truth is his target isn't simply our actions, it's our mind. The war is over control of the way we think. And all too often it feels like he's winning the battle.

A FRIEND asked the typical question: "How are you holding up?" Many others had expressed the same kind of concern. Usually I tried to answer with some cliché that would make me sound more spiritual and closer to God; "Well, you know, I am just surrendering it all."

With this friend it was different. She knows me well and wouldn't accept such a canned response. Honesty was the only option with her: "It just feels like I am being punished—AGAIN—for fathering a child out of wedlock." The words came from the heart and then it was time to ask a question of my own. "How long is God going to hold the past over my head?"

My friend shook her head. It looked like there was pity, like she understood. But then her tone changed. It went from sympathy to attack mode. "That kind of sounds like it's coming from the enemy."

I bristled when the final word came out of her mouth. It was my natural reaction to this kind of talk. But this time the subject wasn't easily discarded. I knew there was a lot of truth to what she was saying.

If a relationship with Jesus is centered in transformation, in moving forward, in changing our identity and modeling our character into something that resembles His, then by contrast the exact opposite must also be true. Satan doesn't want us to change. Instead he's trying to get us to stay put, to embrace the very identity that we're trying to escape. He wants the promise of tomorrow to get lost in the reality of yesterday.

WHAT ABOUT YOU?

1. Describe a time when you lacked faith in yourself, and your own ability to understand and hear when God was reaching out to you?

2. Think of a Christian you are currently in conflict with. If that person were to turn to God and pray about the situation, what would they say?

3. In what way does the enemy attack your thoughts? Is there something in your current circumstance where you are looking at it from his point of view and not from God's?

24

GRADUALLY TO PEACE

I spent the evening before the custody hearing at a neighborhood park. It's a place that holds special meaning for me. It's kind of like the epicenter of my spiritual life. It's where my world was shaken to its core but also where everything finally started to come together.

Four years earlier, on a phone call, I officially got dumped while sitting on a bench here. Only a few days later at the adjacent pool, an intrusive stranger invited me to his church.

The park looked so much like it did on my first visit that I had to wonder if anything really changed. The slide, the swings, the tennis courts were identical. Perhaps I was, too. Once again my life was in chaos with my future hanging in the balance.

A few moments after my arrival, a family of four rolled up on their bikes. Mom and dad were joined by a boy roughly my son's age and his kid sister. "Who invited them?" I said to myself. That father had it made. I hated him! He had everything I wanted. And now, with it right in front of my face, it seemed so far away.

I had to look in another direction. If only there were someone worse off than me. It was a practice in pop psychology. Maybe I could find a poor soul in a wheelchair, or someone horribly disfigured. At least then I could say, “Thank God you’re not in his shoes.” But no one matching such a description was available.

A thought jumped into my head seemingly from out of nowhere. It was of a Biblical story that normally provides comfort, but now it was convicting me. A group of freelance workers are hired in a vineyard. Some are there all day, others join in at lunch time, a few start late in the afternoon, and still more come on right before sunset. At the end of the day, they all get paid the same.

People who come to Christ later in life cling to that parable. It’s the promise that all salvation has the same value. But what if the story is about something else? What if it’s a warning about the sin of comparison?

Like the workers who complained about the pay structure, here I was looking at the father and wondering why things were so unfair. Why did he have it so easy? Why did God bless his life in ways that he neglected my own?

Searching for someone to pity wasn’t any better. Perhaps it was even worse, like I was implying that somehow, because of their circumstances, God loved them less.

The story didn’t stay long in my mind. My brain was on rapid fire. An idea would come in only to be immediately replaced by something else. I wondered what would happened if I lost the custody hearing? How would I spin it to my friends? Did I do something to deserve this? Should I, in the worst case scenario, just pick up and follow everyone to Louisiana?

Then came the answers. I was reminded of the husband and wife who lied about their money and the lesson that truth is more important than image. Lazarus’ sisters made a brief appearance, just long enough to tell me not to search for the reasons behind the pain, but to look for the results. And no matter the outcome, I knew I was supposed to stay put all because Jesus refused to jump from the temple.

The back and forth, rat-a-tat-tat, was clearing something up. Until now, living in peace could only happen when there were no battles to be fought. But maybe peace can exist in the middle of a conflict. All it takes is finding the presence of God.

He was here with me tonight: in His words and through His stories. And with that knowledge it felt like the definition of faith was being altered again. It no longer was about believing in myself. Instead it was in the ability to see this—even this—(the possibility of my worst fear coming true,) as His doing and part of His plan.

Perhaps the word will continue to transform and change meaning. If so, I'll adjust. Because a life of faith requires the ability to keep searching for the truth—even after you found it.

The family was getting back on their bikes and heading home. It was time for me to go, too. It didn't matter anymore that the park looked the same. I knew the change inside of me was real. The broken man who first came here had vanished. Never again would "The Old Doug" be compared to the new one. Somewhere along the way, we had become one and the same.

The future was still unknown. Part of me was nervous, part of me was scared. But there was also an undeniable feeling of hope. Most of all, as the journey had started towards whatever was next; I knew I wasn't leaving alone. And because He was there, with me, I could go in peace.

POSTSCRIPT

ENDURANCE

"We can rejoice, too, when we run into problems and trials, for we know that they are good for us—they help us learn to endure. And endurance develops strength of character in us, and character develops hope. And hope in the end will not disappoint. For we know how dearly God loves us."
(Romans 5:3- 5:5)

GUT CHECK

Part of me wanted to end this book on the previous page. I didn't want the key point to get lost in translation. Time has a way of reducing faith into nothing more than facts.

If you have any doubt about this then go ask your parents how they met. "I saw this beautiful woman across the room…." Your dad may be able to paint the scene but there's no way he can really share the nervousness, the fear of rejection, the incredible courage it took him to walk over and make an introduction. Where's the suspense? The story is about the two people who gave you life. The fact that you're listening to it is a pretty good indicator that somehow it all worked out.

When my pastor preaches on the topic of trust, he usually talks about a time when the church had to make a tough choice. They had a chance to move out of the middle school into a place of their own. This was always the dream, but in order to make it come, true they had to check their gut and take a deep breath. The move was not only expensive but also a very risky undertaking. How it all came together is an amazing account, with twist and turns. Now it's horribly anti-climatic. Because these days when he gives the sermon, my pastor is standing on stage, in the auditorium of the very building once in question. Everyone in the room already knows there's a happy ending.

And so, in order to protect the sense of fear that always comes with trust, part of me wants to leave you hanging. And I would—if only it weren't so cruel.

Indeed what happened with the custody case was very important to my role as a father. But to the follower, what really matters is the faith that got me through it all. It sustained me not just in court, but for a long time afterwards. The hearing ended with the judge promising to look everything over and get back to us…which he eventually did but not until fifty-four days had come and gone.

Waiting takes a lot out of you.

Who knows, maybe God was trying to test me. Actually I hate that word—testing. Christians use it all the time. Heck, the Bible uses it, too. Still, that word just bothers me. It gives the impression that faith is based on what we know or that the outcome will be determined on a pass/fail basis.

I prefer the word "exam" or "examination." The long wait was just God's way of putting my strengths and weaknesses under the microscope. In order to show how deep the roots of my faith had grown, it was necessary for Him to shake things up a bit. Of course the turmoil also revealed those areas that still needed attention.

After four years of calling myself a Christian, my initial knee-jerk reaction hadn't changed that much. The moment anything goes wrong (like when I got the text message), my first response has always been to cut bait, give up and go at it alone.

But I also learned that faith is not defined on impulse. The strength comes from the endurance that continues to engage in the process. Being a Christian is as simple as Jesus, but as the fifty-four days taught me it is also as complex as the reality that we have to pick Him again and again and then again.

Each morning during that seemingly endless stretch of time, I'd surrender all my fears and concerns over to Him. And then the phone would go off, each ring bringing back a layer of tension and nervousness—until the caller I.D. told me it was someone other than the lawyer. And then the process had to start all over from the top: to choose His compassion, His mercy, His kindness, to love "thy enemy" and to place my trust in Him. Not in evidence, testimony or the legal system, but to trust Him.

When the wait was over, the judge decided it was in my son's best interest to live with his father.

Even though that's what I wanted and desired—and on some level why I went searching for God in the first place—by no means is it the end. Not for me. Not for my walk. This was not the destination. It was just a step along the way.

Ultimately my story is like anyone else's. It's about a God who moved from having a chosen people to choosing all peoples. Including those lost sheep that were foolish enough to try to go about life on their own.

Now He's restored us, brought us back to the flock, and given us the assignment to write our own chapters in the story of faith—by worshiping Him and by being His children, the brothers and sisters of Jesus who were sent by the Father and lead by His Spirit.

The Word became flesh, so that all our flesh will become words that speak of His faithfulness and love. Because what started on the Cross, becomes even more amazing each time a new believer stands up and gives an account of his personal resurrection.

You've just read my version of that story. Maybe one day I'll read about yours.

ACKNOWLEDGEMENTS

"I thank God every time I remember you. In all my prayers for all of you, I always pray with joy." Philippians 1:4

There is no such thing as a self made man, and there is no such thing as a single authored book. The words here are mine, but the finished project is really the work of a number of people who encouraged and supported me along the way.

First off, I am honored by those who allowed me to share part of their stories with the reader. Ryan, Karin, Kathy, Jessica, and Rob Campbell all appear in the book because of the impact they've had on my walk. They've helped me grow and allowed my roots to take form.

So many times along the way I wanted to quit this project. And I would have, without the feedback of friends. I benefited from both their kudos and criticisms. Kristen Holt, Gina Rubenstein, Dave Wilstermann, Cheryl Michelet, Tracie Nolde, Tim Blevins, and Heather Kyle read the earlier chapters and told me to keep going.

There are others I need to single out. The key roles of getting this book to print were played by members of my family at Port City Community Church. Kristy Ondo served as the proofreader, Katy Davis was the editor, Kelly Cain Smith designed the cover, and Jesse Stephenson took the photograph on the back. It's impossible to explain my level of gratitude for what they did. Simply put, when you have a dream, in order for it to succeed, it's essential to find people who will invest their own talents and energy to the project. These folks did. And because of their time and energy, they have made me look much better than I deserve.

I thank my friend Holland Graham for her honesty. After reading the original version, she instantly started to nag me, and nag me, and *NAG* me. She wanted me to pick the project back up and rework it. She told me I could make it better. Without her, this book would still be in a desk drawer.

My parents and family need to be mentioned here. When I was leaving my job to pursue this book, they never lectured me on the economy or openly questioned my sanity. They knew I was going in the direction that God desired—and that was enough for them. "Faith, hope and love." You want to know why love is most important? Because without it, faith and hope would remain stagnant. Love is necessary to take the next step and that's what my family provided to this process.

My pastor, Mike Ashcraft, not only wrote the foreword for this book, he's the reason I took up the project in the first place. He's read each chapter along the way and has invested a great amount time in the project. To some degree I will always hold him on a pedestal, because you want your pastor to be the real thing—and mine is. But through this process, Mike has also become a friend and I am truly grateful for that too.

And finally there is Richie Marshall—my mentor—the former beer distributor. He's been a part of this since the very beginning. We used to meet for lunch every Tuesday and he'd let me pick his brain on a variety of Biblical issues that I was taking on in the book. He never preached, never pushed his own agenda, never showed frustration or became argumentative.

Instead, he had the confidence in his faith to allow me to figure things out on my own. He has been a mentor, an ambassador, and most importantly, a friend. The highest compliment I can pay him is by saying that one day I truly hope that I can be someone else's Richie.

On occasion, throughout this process, I have gotten carried away with the fantasy of this becoming a bestseller. But regardless of what happens next, when I think of the people who have helped me along the way, I realize that I have already been filled with a richness that some wealthy men would not understand.

One Drop Media
Wilmington, NC USA

51395
9 780615 445038